Bringing Your Self to Life

Changing Co-Dependent Patterns

Bringing Your Self to Life

Changing Co-Dependent Patterns

Cheryl Hetherington, Ph.D.

Rudi Publishing

Iowa City, Iowa

Rudi Publishing, 1901 Broadway, Suite 321, Iowa City, Iowa 52240

Library of Congress Catalog Card Number: 89-62813.

ISBN 0-945-213-01-8

First Edition, September 1989

PRINTED IN THE UNITED STATES OF AMERICA

Additional copies may be ordered from:
Hetherington & Associates
P.O. Box 367
Iowa City, Iowa 52244

Contents

There is no perfection, but rather progress.

—*Cheryl Hetherington*

Preface

The stories and case studies used throughout this book are composites of couples and individuals with whom I have worked or whom I have known over the years. The specifics and details of the stories, such as names, job descriptions, or geographic locations, have been changed for the purposes of anonymity. You may recognize yourself in a story, or the descriptions may resemble someone you know because in co-dependency there are common patterns and behaviors.

There are countless dysfunctional patterns, and by no means do the stories in this book exemplify all the possible dysfunctional patterns or symptoms that can occur. I have shared stories that show some common patterns learned in dysfunctional families and in a society that encourages an other-centered existence, so that you can get a feel for the types of behaviors that may cause undue pain in your life.

This book is for you. It is not for someone in your life who has an addiction, such as your lover, husband, wife, friend, boss, coworker, or brother. It is to help you with co-dependent patterns that have allowed you to maintain an entanglement with others who have addiction problems. *It is about the inner self-focus which will help you begin to see the patterns that keep you in a position of reacting to someone or something else, rather than to your own needs and wishes.*

Although this book may be of help in understanding and beginning the recovery process, recovery is not something that can be accomplished alone. In many cases it cannot be done without professional help. The information here must be a part of your comprehensive program of recovery.

1. What Co-Dependency Is

Do you feel best when someone needs you?
Do you hear yourself finishing others' sentences for them?
Do you feel that although friends like you, they really don't
    know you?
Have you stayed in an unfulfilling relationship because your
    partner wouldn't be able to take care of himself without
    you?
Do you think, If I want it done right, I have to do it myself?

If you answered yes to any of these questions, you have some degree of co-dependency. This book will explain co-dependency and the characteristics of co-dependent people, along with the family and cultural rules that teach you co-dependent patterns. The last chapter will discuss how you can change these patterns and ways you can transform your life to become more accepting of and comfortable with your own needs and goals.

I became conscious of my own co-dependent patterns many years ago. My sweetie at that time had left me to return to a previous flame: I was hurting and constantly thought about my former partner. Although I did not realize it at the time, this was the third chemically dependent love interest for me. I was totally immersed in thinking about what my former partner was doing. I thought, What is wrong with this person? Why isn't it clear how much I did for our relationship and how much I cared? Surely my friend would see our split as a mistake and return to me. As this self-righteous attitude persisted, friends began to say to me again and again, "You could be thinking about yourself and what you want to be doing, and not about this other person." I shrugged this off. I did manage to go to Al-Anon with them. Slowly, I began to see that I was obsessed with how this person felt about me, and that I was not concerned about how I felt about myself. I had given away all my power by letting another person's actions and feelings determine my self-worth. I was very co-dependent.

1

Another characteristic of co-dependency is an overdeveloped sense of responsibility, for which the co-dependent person may be highly rewarded. Employers think you are terrific because you do what you are told, work extra hard, and go above and beyond the call of duty. You have emerged as a successful-appearing adult. So why try to change? Isn't responsibility a great thing? More is better, right? Aren't you supposed to care more for others than for yourself? What is wrong with this noble way of life? The answer is that there is dishonesty and pain under the façade of the "noble" caretaker.

While feeling depressed and sad one winter, I did not have much energy and had little interest in my work. As my depression lifted, I told my supervisor that I was feeling better and thought I could do a better job now and be more pleasant to others. Although a perceptive person, he said that he had not noticed a change and that I seemed to be as cheerful as usual. As I considered this, I realized that there was a large gap between how I felt and how I presented myself at work. I kept up the cheery façade even when I felt like crying. I kept plodding away, without giving myself some time to work through my sadness consistently and honestly. This is one of many characteristic behaviors of co-dependency.

I learned that the word *co-dependency* describes a pattern of beliefs, learned behaviors, and habitual feelings that make life painful. Others may see a "together," successful image, but the "real" person inside is insecure, feels like a failure, and can be dangerously self-neglectful or even self-destructive. *Co-dependency is a distressful way of coping with life that makes people more dependent on things outside themselves than they have to be.* I learned that I spent so much time managing and controlling work and relationships that I had little time left for myself.

There are degrees in the continuum of co-dependency. In the early phase there are feelings of hurt, sadness, and fear, and the mildly co-dependent person will make excuses or deny that anything is wrong. You might hear yourself saying to a child, "Your dad has been very busy lately, and I am sure he will be very sorry that he missed your graduation." You may be a compulsive cleaner and keep your home spotless. While you look organized and neat on the outside, on the inside you may be scared and feel confused or angry. Your thoughts and feelings may be unorganized and seem to be a mass of confusion. There are contradictions between your feelings and your behavior. You may live in a world of denial where you tell yourself that things really aren't so bad. You learn not to feel what you cannot tolerate.

Extreme cases of co-dependency may be marked by feelings of shame, depression, and emptiness. People at this stage feel they have nothing to live for, nothing positive to look forward to. They feel hopeless and helpless. They cling to relationships, and they will do anything to avoid abandonment. Symptoms of extreme co-dependence include suicide attempts, general depression, and chronic physical illness. Co-dependency is progressive; it can be increasingly serious and eventually life-threatening if you do not attend to the symptoms.

2. Characteristics of Co-Dependent People

Co-dependent people have many distinguishing characteristics, and all of them involve being excessively other-centered—that is, being concerned with someone or something other than their own thoughts and feelings. Co-dependents have excessive concern with how others behave, dress, eat, spend money. A neighbor of mine looked carefully at my clothes each time she saw me. She would look at me, head to toe, her eyes and head moving vertically a few times, as she checked out what I was wearing that day. Then she might say, "Oh, you have on that skirt from the L. L. Bean catalog," or "I'll bet you got that blouse on sale downtown at Hazel's dress shop." She was constantly looking at and thinking about what I and everyone else wore each day. Her interest was focused on public image and appearance, and she paid attention to clothes. She spent little time attending to her inner life. This is one of many characteristics of co-dependent people.

Losing Contact

People who are co-dependent lose contact with their own needs, goals, and feelings when an outside development, like a new relationship, seems to demand top priority. Pat was in a managerial position at a university, and she had plans to go back to school to study in a specialty area. As she was collecting information about her options, she fell in love with someone who lived three hours away from her. As Pat began to see her new lover regularly, she became confused about her goals and missed the application deadlines for her carefully selected programs. She began to talk of going to school in the town where her new lover lived, even though the program there had little to offer in her specialty. To support herself in this new place, she considered applying for a student assistantship in a department where she was actually qualified for a top-level management position. She was willing to compromise all her plans, to go to school in a program that had little to offer her, and to work at a job she had held ten years previously. This extensive accommodation for a three-month-old relationship nearly immobilized Pat, and she was unable to remember, let alone act on, her previous plan. She lost contact with some of her inner goals and wishes by focusing solely on moving to be with her new love.

Helping and Solving

Co-dependent people satisfy their personal needs by "helping" or trying to "solve" others' problems. This behavior is the "band-aid" or "fix-it" syndrome. It is easy to recognize a person who has the fix-it syndrome. When you are telling her about a problem you have, she listens to your problem for a short time, then says, "Why don't you . . . ?" It is as if she cannot stand for you to be in distress. She thinks that to be worth her salt, she must offer a solution that will make it all better. She wants to rescue you from your dilemma. However, if you do not take her suggestion, or you tell her you don't want advice, she may think that you do not care about her. Helpers and solvers define their worth by how much they are able to help and solve for others. When the offers of help are rejected, the helper feels rejected as a person, and the act of turning down help becomes a personal injury. The "helper" becomes "victim" and may think, All I try to do is help and all I get is people being mean to me. This kind of co-dependent behavior is often part of the "rescue triangle," which I will discuss later.

Taking Care of Others/Being Needed

Some people cannot distinguish between caring *for* and taking *care of*, or between being responsible *to* and responsible *for*. There is confusion between nurturance of another and intimacy with another. One way to show your friends that you care about them is to listen to them and acknowledge their feelings when they tell you or show you. Then you share your own feelings with them. You can be *responsible to* them by being honest about your feelings. This is intimacy.

Nurturance is different. It is doing nice things for another. Nurturance is very valuable and all of us appreciate and need nurturance in our lives. Co-dependents are so intent on taking care of or nurturing others that sometimes they try to protect people from their own responsibilities. You may try to *take care of* your friend by doing something for her that you think she wants. If your friend is afraid to tell your mutual boss that she has broken a piece of equipment in the office, you may tell the boss that it is broken and

5

deny knowing how it was broken. This is trying to *take care of* your friend and her responsibility. You do not distinguish between where your responsibilities end and your friend's responsibilities begin.

Trying to take care of others leads to confusion between being needed and being loved and is a common characteristic of co-dependent adults. Joan thought that she could not leave a relationship because her partner could not get along without her. She believed she had total control over and responsibility for her partner's well-being. She was confused about what love was: she was needed and therefore thought she was loved. She thought that if she left her partner, he would start taking drugs again and overdose. She said, "If I am there, I can keep him from taking drugs. I have to control the situation." Eventually Joan's feelings of being trapped and dishonest became so painful she left the relationship anyway. She and her former partner survived.

Much later Joan realized that her focus on her partner was a way to avoid her own feelings and needs. She had learned as a child that loving meant helping others and that her own needs were secondary. As an adult she did not recognize her own feelings (many of which were painful) because she had sought out others who were more than willing to accept all the care and attention they could get from her. Once she was able to become focused on her own needs and goals, she did not like or want to be in this kind of a relationship. She realized that being needed was not the same as being loved.

Being Perfect

Some co-dependent people try to be perfect, to have a perfect house, job, lover, child, or other evidence of being in control. When you try to control your environment so that it appears that you are perfect, you are usually most concerned with what others will think of you. This behavior is called *impression management.* It happens when you concentrate on impressing or pleasing others. When you are highly invested in how others see you, you have little awareness of how you really feel.

When I know that a friend is coming over and I am *not* worried about cleaning up the magazines in the living room, that friend is someone I trust and someone I have allowed to know me. I am not concerned that she will care what the living room looks like, and I am not holding her at arm's length. The reality is that she is coming over to see me, not to see if I am a good housekeeper. I am not trying to manage and control the impression she has of me.

I am myself, not a pseudo-person presented to make an impression. Striving to be perfect is a way to avoid your own self-awareness.

Isolating

Co-dependent people are socially isolated; they have many acquaintances, but few intimate friends. If you have many friends who do not really know you, you probably do not share your important feelings with them. You do not let yourself be vulnerable to them. It is a lonely place to be if you can't call on others when you need to talk about being scared, sad, or hurt.

Jake is a very popular guy with many acquaintances. He is handsome, in good physical shape, funny, and gregarious. He learned at age six to act responsibly and maturely. He does not show others his real feelings. He does most things in the extreme: he constantly collects records and has over two thousand albums. He lifts weights daily to lose the weight he gains while binge eating. At the age of thirty-two, he first began to allow memories of sexual abuse from his father to emerge. He is lonely, scared, and isolated, and he says no one really knows him. He makes sure of that by making up stories about his life and lying about the smallest things. He is scared to let his feelings emerge from his memory. He believes that he will fall apart and his image of being "all together" will be tarnished. Since the memories are pushing to be remembered, he has started physically isolating himself more so that others will not see him fall apart. As Jake becomes more aware of his frightening feelings, he increasingly isolates himself. Isolation increases as you try to hide feelings and avoid painful memories.

Maintaining a Façade

Co-dependent people have low self-worth, but maintain a cheery façade with others. A very commonly accepted co-dependent ritual is this: You are asked "How are you?"; you answer "Fine." You are probably maintaining a mask of control to cover the variety of feelings that we all have. If you feel sad, hurt, scared, or angry while maintaining this façade, you may feel isolated, dishonest, and bad about yourself. It takes a lot of energy to maintain cheeriness, and you may find you are out of gas in the middle of the day. If underneath the cheerful public image you are self-deprecating, if you question or discount your own perceptions or believe you do not have good judgment, you have low self-worth. It is difficult to be proud of yourself, to accept compliments or gifts. Often when I bring my friend Laura a gift of flowers or a small token of appreciation, she says, "Oh, you didn't have to do that." She is unable to accept the gift fully because she believes she doesn't deserve it. Her self-worth is low, and she does not know what to say when others are kind to her. Although she is friendly and cheerful, Laura feels unworthy of gifts or appreciation from others.

Being Alone

The fear of being alone is common for co-dependent people, and they have difficulty being spontaneous, letting go, and having fun without drugs or alcohol. Tim, age thirty-four, would do anything to avoid being alone. He worked long hours, then would stop on the way home to get a six-pack of beer for the evening. He stayed in the college town where he went to school and often dated younger college women. When I asked him what he liked about the woman he was dating, he said she was someone to be with and she didn't mind having sex with him. He did not really like her; in fact, he thought she was rather immature and uninteresting, yet he went to the college bars with her because he was afraid to be alone. He continued to see her because she filled the scary empty spaces in his life. Alone, Tim might have to face his own feelings. Companionship and alcohol shifted his focus and responsibility away from himself. He became increasingly depressed and said, "I feel like my life has little meaning." It is no wonder, considering that he was spending time with this woman and others he did not care about because he was afraid of being alone.

Avoiding Intimacy

The fear of intimacy is common for co-dependent people. You may use alcohol, drugs, or some compulsive behavior to avoid intimacy in relationships. Larry came to see me as he was ending his second marriage. He came from a home where the mother was controlling and wanted to know about everything her children and husband did and said. She viewed any disagreement with her as a personal attack and would cry or pout and claim that no one appreciated her, and that she was only trying to help. Most of the time she was angry or complained of a physical ailment. By the time Larry was a teenager, he was depressed, sullen, and involved with drugs and alcohol. Although he had many friends and usually a girlfriend, he did not feel close to anyone. His older sister was the family heroine. She made good grades, worked hard, did what was asked, and appeared to have everything under control. She was a hard act for Larry to follow. Larry first married Jane, who was a heavy marijuana smoker, did not have a job, had little education, but knew how to have fun and laugh. She brought laughter and some playfulness into Larry's life. She was also very possessive and jealous. Larry had fun with Jane, but they did not talk about their feelings and shared little intimacy. Although Larry felt obligated to take care of Jane, especially after she had an abortion, he did not feel safe with Jane. They both smoked marijuana on a regular basis and spent little time together when they were not high.

After a few years, Larry and Jane divorced, although Jane followed him around and threatened him with violence. Larry was scared and just wanted to get away from her. He began to drink more and more, attempted suicide several times, and was depressed and lonely for a few years. Although his family made a halfhearted attempt to get him into alcohol and drug treatment, he did not go for help.

At a low point in his life, he met Peg through a mutual friend. At this same time, he found religion and decided it was bad to drink and use drugs. So Larry stopped using recreational drugs, although he continued taking prescription drugs for his chronic, injury-induced back pain. Peg and Larry had a good time together, and he especially enjoyed the sexual part of their relationship. It was not evident to Larry until a few years after they were married that Peg was another controlling woman who fluctuated between being helpless and wanting more—more food, a bigger home, another car. Once again, Larry was with a woman with whom he could avoid intimacy. To maintain order in his environment, Larry had become very neat and could not tolerate a disorderly home, so he kept the home spotless even though Peg was fairly sloppy. He worked harder and harder to make money to buy the things Peg wanted. Larry had become more and more cut off from himself. He continued to take narcotics for his back pain, which became so unbearable at times that he was unable to work. He was in crisis most of the time in the ten years of his marriage to Peg. He was estranged from his family, angry and depressed, addicted to narcotics, and enmeshed in his relationship with Peg.

When Peg asked him for a divorce, he was at first very resistant and terrified that he would be alone. After a few months, however, he began to seek alternative treatment for his back, stopped taking medication, moved out of the house, and began to talk to his friends and family again. He had realized that he was on a fast track to an early death and needed to clean up his act. However, in his constant search for intensity and avoidance of intimacy with others, he next became enthralled with his new diet and exercise treatment. As the new plan helped him become pain- and drug-free, he said that he needed to work on his need for perfection. Larry's need for order and the perfect house, car, etc., were his blocks to intimacy.

Fearing Abandonment and Unexpected Changes

Co-dependent people fear abandonment and unexpected changes. When Ed first met his partner, he tried to become integrated into her group of friends. Although he did not smoke marijuana, he often joined her friends as they sat around the kitchen table, smoking dope, talking and laughing. Ed accommo- dated to their behavior because he was afraid that his new romantic interest and her friends wouldn't like him if he didn't. He had learned this pattern in response to earlier childhood fears of being abandoned and had unconsciously accommodated because of these fears.

In his family, Ed was the oldest and the harmonizer or the peacekeeper. He was the one who did the dishes when his sister did not do them, so that his mother would not be mad. He accom- modated to other family members' needs to avoid the comments of a mother who was often critical and generally not appreciative of her family's efforts. Now an adult, Ed fears that he cannot be funny and interesting unless he smokes with the group, accommo- dating to them as he had to his family. It is common to accommo- date to new friends or to a new love's life in the beginning, yet when this behavior continues, you can become less and less attentive to your own needs and interests. Ed continues to do whatever his new partner wants and says, and he does not share many of his own wishes with her. Although he says he has some of his own interests, he would rather be with her and do what she likes.

If you give up activities that you enjoy but your partner or spouse does not like, you may become resentful and lose your sense of yourself as an individual person with important needs and interests separate from your partner or spouse. Because of Ed's fear of abandonment, he has never developed a clear sense of himself and is unaware of or inattentive to his own needs and interests. He abandons himself for the sake of the relationship, whether with family, friends, or a significant other.

Loving Adequately

Believing yourself unable to love adequately is part of the co-dependent pattern. Kathy chose men who were domineering and controlling, and she went along with whatever they wanted to do. She thought this would show them that she really cared about them. When asked where she wanted to go to dinner, she would reply, "I don't care; any place is all right with me." She had little sense of herself. After being involved with a man for a few weeks, she began to get angry at him; she felt he did not care about her because he was content doing everything his way. She felt lonely and empty, and she realized she did not care about him either. Then she became depressed and withdrawn, and she came to the conclusion that she did not know how to love adequately, and the relationship failure was her fault. After this happened several times, Kathy decided that she would not get involved at all because there must be something wrong with her. For several years Kathy avoided romantic relationships with men.

Avoiding Conflict

Co-dependent people go to great lengths to avoid conflict. Later they feel anger and resentment. At age thirty-six, Sandy had been married to James for sixteen years. She had grown up on a ranch in the Southwest and loved dogs, yet lived in the city with James. She worked at odd jobs, but mostly raised their three children and maintained a cheery façade with her many acquaintances. She had no close friends and she was miserable inside, but felt she should be thankful for the expensive house and many nice things her husband provided for her. They were James's way of showing his love for her. An introverted and quiet man, he had difficulty talking about his feelings and felt his presence was enough to let her know that he cared about her. Sandy did not like conflict, but longed for the country and a ranch where she could train dogs. At one point she left home for several months for an affair with another man, simply because he had show dogs and she could help him groom and train them. When that relationship did not work out, she was warmly welcomed home by her husband, who adored her and was glad to have her back. To prove how glad, he provided capital for a ranch where Sandy could begin a dog-training business, although he feared that she would not spend time on keeping up the house, or with him and the children. That is exactly what happened. To avoid conflict, she claimed that in order to build her business, she must spend a lot of time working on it. Sandy loved what she was doing and had redirected her energy to the dogs and the people she hired. She spent very little time with her husband, but was unable to tell him about her anger and hurt feelings. She was a gregarious and lively person but often went to great lengths to avoid conflict. Rather than face the conflicts Sandy knew were inevitable if she were honest, she avoided her husband as much as possible.

Taking Life Seriously

Co-dependent people take life and themselves very seriously and are always struggling to be better—better lovers, better managers, or better tennis players. I once worked with a person who was very serious, rarely smiled or laughed, and worked long hours to become more skilled at her profession. She would do anything for you, and always *seriously* wanted to know if there was something else she could do to help you. When I suggested to her that she needed to relax, have some fun, go dancing, or play a little, she responded, "I *have been working on relaxing* for several months now." For her, everything was work, and usually there was no time left to play. When there was, she worked very hard at enjoying herself. Her seriousness made spontaneous fun and playfulness difficult.

Being Concerned about What Others Think

People who are co-dependent are excessively concerned with what others think, want, and need. As "pleasers," they are usually very perceptive about what others need and will try to provide for these needs so that others will like them. As perceptive observers, they will be the first to pass the salt at the dinner table when someone simply looks up in a visual search for the salt shaker. This kind of behavior usually does result in rewards in our culture—praise, attention, and appreciation. Some co-dependents may become stubborn about knowing what others want without asking directly and thus set themselves up for rejection by forcing their "gifts" or "help" inappropriately.

Co-dependent people can tolerate only approval or "positive vibes." They are often experts at avoiding or derailing conflict. A friend with whom I once worked teased and made jokes at staff meetings as soon as others began to disagree with what she was saying, and soon the topic was lost. Sometimes she backed down to avoid a confrontation. In her own mind, if someone disagreed with her, he did not like her, and her coworkers' approval was more important to her than any of the ideas she presented.

Tolerating Inappropriate Behavior

Co-dependent people have a high tolerance for inappropriate behavior from others. They often marry alcoholics or some other type of addict and put up with a host of behaviors that seem highly inappropriate to less co-dependent people. Tilly worked hard on the night shift as a nurse in a hospital. At home she cleaned, cooked, did laundry and grocery shopping, paid the bills, and did anything else that needed to be done around the house. Her husband worked at odd jobs, spent much of his time at bars during the evening, and slept much of the day. He often took money out of their checking account to go to the racetrack or to go drinking. When confronted about the missing money, he would tell Tilly that he had used it to fix the car. Although she doubted his story, she would say only, "I just can't count on him." For years she put up with lying, lots of hangovers, little personal attention, and no financial assistance. Tilly tolerated inappropriate behavior for many years by explaining to others that her husband was having a hard time and needed her support.

Avoiding Compliments and Criticism

Co-dependent people often dismiss compliments and are wounded by criticism. As an overachiever, I thought that I could always do more and do it better the next time. When I got evaluations from my boss, typically they included lots of praise and encouragement. Sometimes there was a suggestion for improvement or change. At the bottom of one glowing evaluation it said, "Would like to see you more often at informal meetings. Let's stay in better contact." Later that day when someone asked me how my evaluation meeting went, I said, "My boss thinks that I am not cooperating with him enough." I did not remember the first page of praise, only the minor suggestion for change. As I look back, I realize that he probably missed the occasional lunches we had had together the year before, and that he wanted to make at least one suggestion to motivate me to keep up the good work. I had dismissed the compliments and looked for any hint of criticism.

Participating in the Rescue Triangle

Co-dependent people are often engaged in the *rescue triangle*, in which they switch from rescuer to victim to persecuter, depending on the situation. One friend who was uncomfortable with others' distress felt compelled to try to fix the situation when others complained about something that bothered them. Rhonda worked in an agency that provided food service for a hotel. She was bright, funny, and a hard worker. She was well liked and had a lot of innovative ideas for improvement of the agency. Whenever other women in her work group complained about a problem, she was the first to offer a suggestion for change and to try to help take care of the problem. It was important to her to please other people, and she could do this by trying to fix things for others.

One day a coworker, Paula, came to Rhonda and said, "I just don't know how I am going to get all the vendor orders completed in time to pick up my daughter from daycare today." Rhonda said, "No problem, I will help you till you get them done." Paula was delighted, and Rhonda started working on the orders to rescue Paula. While Paula spent much of the rest of the day complaining to others about how much work she had to get done, Rhonda continued to work on the orders. When 5:00 P.M. rolled around, Rhonda was still working on the orders and Paula quickly left, without a thank-you or an acknowledgment of Rhonda's help. Rhonda was steaming mad as she was left there with the orders still incomplete.

While Rhonda started out being a *rescuer*, she now felt like a *victim*. She felt that she was not appreciated and had been used by Paula. The rescue triangle was complete the next day when Rhonda started complaining to others about how lazy and unorganized Paula is at work. Rhonda had now become the *persecutor*. She expressed her anger and resentment by criticizing Paula, who could not get her own work done and who did not appreciate Rhonda's help enough to thank her properly. Rhonda, in her efforts to jump in to save Paula from her own responsibilities, participated in the "grand trio," the rescuer-victim-persecutor triangle.

Fusing and Distancing

Co-dependent people vacillate between fusion and distancing in intimate relationships. Lee was very friendly and kind to others, yet few people knew her very well. She did not reveal much about herself and kept a distance between herself and others. She very carefully selected what she said to others until she met a man with whom she felt vulnerable. Then she would spill her heart out, telling him everything she felt and thought. Sometimes this scared others away from her and she then felt abandoned and resentful. Other times she realized too late that she'd become intimate with someone she didn't like or couldn't trust. Lee had a difficult time with moderation in intimate relationships; she vacillated between intimacy and distance, equating intimacy with fusion. You may tell "too much to too many, too often" and experience fusion, while other times you do not let anyone know your feelings, thus maintaining a distance.

Connecting and Separating

In *Dance of Intimacy* Harriet Lerner talks about navigating the connectedness (we) and the separateness (I). Often this is a matter of knowing your own desires, wishes, or needs and having the ability to define your own comfortable, personal, emotional boundaries or limits. Emma, a lesbian, had been in a relationship with Mary for two years; they lived around the corner from another lesbian couple, Judy and Sharon. They were all friends and spent considerable social time together. Emma was very hurt when her partner, Mary, told her that she was in love with Judy. The troublesome part of this situation was that Mary expected Emma to pretend that everything was well in their relationship to protect Judy from facing the truth with Sharon and others among their friends. Emma did keep Mary's secret and felt it was another way to show Mary that she loved her.

However, Emma was putting Mary's needs ahead of her own. She was very sad, not eating or sleeping well, and was in a depression. She needed to talk about her feelings and thus came to see me. As we talked, she realized that she did not have a clear sense of her own boundaries and limits in this situation nor, in fact, in general. Later, it became clear that Mary had become less interested in the relationship, feeling smothered, because Emma had lost a sense of her own direction. Emma was unable to separate herself from the needs and wishes of Mary and had little sense of herself as a separate person (I) in the relationship. Having the relationship was more important than having a sense of her own self. She felt fused and had functioned as a connected person (we). She was unclear about her own boundaries and was willing to be dishonest to protect Mary and Judy for a while during the early part of their new relationship.

Intimacy became a problem for Emma after a hurtful ending with Mary. She was unwilling to get close to others for several years. The grieving she did during that time was an important element in regaining her separateness and identity as an individual. She forgave Mary and forgave herself and was able to maintain a close and loving friendship with Mary. However, she was fearful of entering into other intimate (not necessarily sexual) relationships with people. She valued her separateness and was afraid that in an intimate relationship she would lose the ability to maintain her "I-ness."

You may become disconnected from yourself or others when you are told by your family that your feelings are not valid and you should not talk about them. You learn to ignore or *disconnect* from your feelings. You may also learn to avoid any feelings for others so that you can maintain emotional distance from them. When a child or an adult is prevented from participating in mutually responsive or mutually enhancing relationships, serious disconnections may occur. These disconnections happen in dysfunctional families when the child or adult is grossly abused or attacked. Jean Baker Miller says that disconnection occurs when "the surrounding relational context is unresponsive to the child or adult's expression of her experience."[1] When you were a child, people may not have listened to you, told you that "there is nothing to cry about," to "put a lid on it" (you cannot be angry here), that you were crazy for loving or liking someone. If these disconnections happen consistently over time, you may learn not to trust your experience, feelings, or judgments. You may doubt your decisions and experiences. You may begin to believe that something is deeply wrong with you. You are lonely, and you are likely to believe that it is your fault that you are disconnected and left out of the group of people in the world who are in the know. You may feel helpless, powerless, unable to act to change the situation. Alice Lawler says that "disconnection, when it occurs frequently in a person's life, leads to the inability to nurture oneself or others, the inability to express one's feelings, a sense of confusion about who one is, and a distorted view of oneself and of the world."[2]

If you can identify with several of the characteristics in this chapter, chances are you have a strong outward focus and are not in tune with your personal needs. You are co-dependent to the degree that these characteristics cause problems in your relationships and your general joy and appreciation of life.

---

1. Jean Baker Miller, "Connections, Disconnections, and Violations," work in progress (paper no. 33), Stone Center for Developmental Services and Studies, 1988. Can be ordered from the Stone Center, Wellesley College, Wellesley, MA 02181.

2. Alice Lawler, "The Healthy Self: Variations on a Theme," unpublished paper, 1988, p. 8. Available from Alice Lawler, Counseling and Mental Health Center, University of Texas at Austin, Austin, TX 78713-8119.

3. How You Learn Patterns of Co-Dependency: The Family Rules

People start to learn co-dependent patterns as children. The family is primary among various sources where children learn these patterns. Co-dependency is a method of adaptation to or imitation of a family's style of interaction. Co-dependent families often create highly stressful, unpredictable environments, with many family secrets and rules that prohibit open communication. Members are blamed, compared negatively to others, or called names. For example, a mother may say to her child, "You are just like your stupid father; you don't do anything I tell you." These are hurt words. When you hear these messages from your parents, you internalize the message and learn inappropriate responsibility and low self-esteem. You carry these messages with you into adulthood. Adults who still use childhood coping behaviors which cause more pain than they alleviate are commonly termed "adult children." Many of the characteristics of co-dependency and adult children are the same; using the term "adult children" highlights the origin of the problems they share.

Parents may expect children to assume tasks and responsibilities beyond their maturity level. For example, a six-year-old is expected to call the parent's employer when the parent is too sick to go to work. The child becomes the parent and acts as caretaker for his or her parents. Jake, whose feelings of isolation were discussed earlier, says that he loved being in school and hated weekends, because he and his sister were expected to stay in the house all day every Saturday during his childhood. From age six, both were expected to clean the house—scrub floors, wash clothes, cook, and do all the other household tasks. If they did not do a task to their parents' satisfaction, they would have to do it over with little or no parental assistance; Jake's mother and father would watch TV or sit outside during the summer. Jake and his sister became the caretakers for their parents, and Jake at age thirty-two still tiptoes around them. He tells them very little about his life and protects them from a great deal of the anger he feels towards them. He does express his anger through emotional blackmail. He trades money (charge accounts, a new car) for not bringing up his anger, particularly about the incest that victimized him. Jake's parents would rather pay him off than deal with that.

Co-dependency often develops in families where there is alcoholism, incest, chronic physical or mental illness, or another form of chronic stress. However, no major or obvious family problems are necessary in order for co-dependent behavior to exist. Most often, co-dependent behavior is modeled by parents and grandparents, and this behavior is considered normal even though it creates pain and unhappiness. Dysfunctional families with problems and/or secrets create adult children—and are very common.

In dysfunctional families children may grow up with rules that prevent them from expressing themselves. Claudia Black discusses the DON'T TALK, DON'T TRUST, DON'T FEEL rules, which cause children to deny their feelings so often. They eventually do not know what their feelings are. They may receive so many double (or triple) messages—"Do what I say, not what I do"—they really do not know what is reality and what is fiction. Children can deny that anything is wrong, especially since they don't trust their own judgment. If those in authority around them—parents, teachers, older siblings—say everything is all right, that everything is normal, children believe that everything must be all right. If everything doesn't seem all right, they believe something is wrong with them, or they think they do not have good judgment or are not smart enough.

There are several ways that the DON'T TALK, DON'T TRUST, DON'T FEEL rules are learned. Here are some of the specific rules learned in a home where there is considerable avoidance and denial.[1]

It is not okay to talk about problems.

This is the "Don't talk" rule: where communication is poor, outward expressions of emotion are discouraged. Children learn to ignore their feelings; thus, personal identity and needs come second. They feel as if they are "walking on eggshells." Joel's father worked at night, and he and his sisters were not allowed to talk in the house during the day. His mother would say, "You have

---

1. Claudia Black, *It Will Never Happen to Me!* (Denver: Medical Administration Company Printing and Publications, 1981).

to be quiet while your father is sleeping. If you have something to say, wait until he goes to work tonight." Joel learned that being quiet was more important than his feelings. He learned to blame his dad and did not talk about his feelings to anyone. Joel learned not to share his feelings with anyone and to resent his father. He never has talked to his dad about anything important to him, and he believes his feelings are not important or valid.

Feelings should not be expressed openly.

This rule is learned by hearing things like "I don't know what you are so happy about," or "I'll give you something to cry about." According to this family rule, children learn that it is more acceptable to deny feelings than to express them. As a result of being cut off from their emotions, people often develop physical problems, such as tension headaches, ulcers, rashes, insomnia, and depression; they often "shut down" and do not experience feelings—they do not know how they feel. The mind and the body are closely connected and physical illness is often connected to psychological distress. Feelings will be expressed one way or another; those not directly acknowledged find other channels.

Communication should be indirect.

With the family functioning under this restriction, one family member acts as a messenger between other members. This is called *triangulation*. The child becomes a mediator for the mother and father, trying to patch up arguments. Or the child may provide a buffer so that the parents do not have to talk to each other but can express their anger or resentment through the child. The child is used by the mother or father, or both, to avoid talking face-to-face. Messages get mixed or confused, and the child may blame him- or herself for whatever happens. Co-dependent patterns develop as the child learns not to communicate openly and to feel responsible for others' personal problems. The child learns to try to guess how others feel or what they want.

Be strong, be good, be right, be perfect, make us proud.

With this rule, the parent conveys unrealistic expectations to the child. There is often only one right way to do things in the home, and the child begins to learn that "enough is never enough." For example, the father may want the child to wash and dry the dinner dishes a certain way, and he checks up on the child every few minutes. When the child is finished, the father will find something that is not done to his liking and will either comment on it or do it himself, saying, "Won't you ever learn?" With such a controlling parent, children create an ideal for themselves (to be "picture perfect"), and the ideal is so far removed from what is possible that they end up feeling punished because they do not meet these expectations. To be bound to perfection is to be bound to failure. The child learns that no matter how much or how well she tries to please the parent, it will never be enough. Thus she may become a perfectionist and keep trying, or become depressed, give up altogether, and accept the "fact" that she is "no good."

Do not be selfish.

Under this rule, children learn to view themselves as wrong for placing their own needs before the needs of others. Co-dependents try to feel good about themselves by taking care of others, and eventually their self-esteem becomes dependent on care-taking. Without someone to take care of, the co-dependent is left without purpose or worth. For co-dependents who grow up in a family system where this rule is rigidly applied to every situation, one feeling emerges with certainty—*guilt*.

Do as I say, not as I do.

This rule teaches a child not to trust. Co-dependent children believe that their parents are not honest because they see behavior that is inconsistent with the spoken rules. They begin to protect themselves from the pain of this inconsistency by not trusting at all. For example, a child is punished for stealing a package of gum from the drugstore, yet the child sees that the mother does not tell the grocery-store clerk when an item under the cart is not included in the bill. This is very confusing to the child, and the primary lesson is *Do not trust* your parent. And if you can't trust your parents, whom can you trust? The child often comes up with the obvious answer—I can't trust anyone.

It is not okay to play.

Children in a family with oppressive rules are deprived of the carefree play of childhood—their time is spent taking care of a parent, grandparent, or sibling, or being a mediator. Co-dependent children expect themselves to work twice as hard as everyone else just to feel okay. It becomes increasingly important to their feelings of adequacy that they have something to do *all* the time. Ultimately, they deny their need to play. The more they suffer, the more playing in spontaneous or silly ways is too frightening. Anything spontaneous has the potential of stirring up all those feelings and the pain that is so carefully kept under wraps. When others tell jokes and laugh, the co-dependent person often cautiously watches and does not participate. Play is viewed as a selfish, irresponsible, and useless activity.

You must always look good.

Melody Beattie, in *Beyond Codependency*, refers to this rule. No matter how you feel or what you have to do—always look good. When a mother and teenage daughter are shopping in a mall and each is angry and frustrated with the other, the mother pretends that there is nothing wrong when they happen to meet a relative in the store. The mother talks cheerily about what a great day they are having together. She keeps smiling at her sullen daughter to encourage her to play the game of "let's pretend we are happy with each other"—no matter how mad we are.

The look-good rule also applies to having a nice yard, house, and car, and clean, well-dressed children. This rule is in opposition to being yourself. It keeps you conforming to an abstract, often unrealistic, and potentially unhealthy standard.

Do not rock the boat.

This rule seeks to maintain an unhealthy balance in the family, keeping the family dishonest and keeping the secrets. The boat is the public image of the family as all right, perfect, conforming to all the rules. Differences—such as being honest about disliking Uncle Joe or not eating meat at the Thanksgiving dinner—are not accepted. Then differences become problems. "We don't talk about our problems. We don't show our feelings." The family does not allow any healthy change because it is too frightening. Anything that threatens the "balance" is not allowed or the "boat" will capsize and the world will know that the family is not perfect, that there are terrible secrets.

Gay and lesbian people especially learn this; they know that rocking the boat has grave repercussions. In her book *Permanent Partners*, Betty Berzon says that "the majority of gay and lesbian people grew up with a terrible secret that affected practically everything you did.... Most of us were very much alone with our secret. You couldn't go for help to the people you would usually turn to because you knew, somehow, that they wouldn't like what you had to tell them. So you developed your sense of who you were as sexual beings in a context of confusion and self-deprecation."

Non-gay people who grow up with family secrets know

this rule as well, and typically do not rock the boat. The family secret can be that Dad has a retarded brother somewhere, that sister had an abortion, that Mother takes lots of prescription drugs, that stepfather sexually molests teenage daughters, that Mom drinks and verbally abuses the family, that Dad has affairs, that Aunt Peggy is a lesbian, that brother Jim has AIDS, that Father is depressed, that Dad and brother had a big fight which sent brother off to die in Vietnam. The family goes through complicated and painful gyrations—moving the household, lying to physicians, ending friendships, overworking—to avoid "rocking the boat" and facing the truth. *This rule—Don't rock the boat—oversees and directs all the other rules in the family.*

4. Our Addictive Culture

Thus far, only the family has been discussed as a place where restrictive rules are learned. To stop with the influence of the family is to stop too soon. You are influenced greatly by many sources. In her books, *Co-dependency: Misunderstood—Mistreated* and *Escape from Intimacy*, Anne Wilson Schaef discusses some other sources of restrictive rules: school, churches, the political system, and the society as a whole. In many institutions in our society, there are specific hurtful lessons learned when co-dependency and addiction exist as the norm. Four of these are 1) dishonesty; 2) frozen feelings; 3) thinking disorders; and 4) perfectionism. These will be discussed in view of the addictive problems of our culture.

The American society struggles with addictive problems. John and Linda Friel, in *Adult Children*, list some of the most common agents to which people in our society become addicted; you may know of others:

alcohol	jogging
prescription drugs	reading
nonprescription drugs	speed
illegal drugs	nicotine
food	caffeine
television	relationships
sex	power
work	spending
gambling	stress
cults	danger

These agents are not necessarily addictive in and of themselves. It is the use and abuse of them that creates the addiction. It is the lack of moderation that creates the problem. When anything is excessively used to avoid intimacy or deny feelings, override an inability to let go, mask inner torment or insecurity, or cover other inner problems, there exists the basis for addiction. Addiction is *over-*

extended involvement with the agent or activity. The addictive process can take many forms, and it always includes the elements of avoidance and denial.

The addicted person may seem in control. That control is an illusion. When you are doing something to avoid or deny your feelings, you are not in control of your life. Whatever you are doing or whatever agent you are using is in control of your life. The "Don't rock the boat" rule of the family can be the internal rule for an organization or a society as well as for an individual. It becomes critically important not to let feelings, pain, and problems surface. The way to accomplish that becomes an addiction: drinking, gambling, working, cleaning, taking care of someone else, exercising, taking risks. Cultural encouragement for this kind of over-extension includes television advertisements showing only happy, beautiful, trouble-free people in bars drinking alcohol; corporations that reward with promotions and perks those employees who work fifty to sixty hours per week; the cultural gods and goddesses of exercise encouraging us via video to look like them . . . which for them is a full-time job. The four lessons—dishonesty, frozen feelings, thinking disorders, and perfectionism—encourage co-dependent patterns in our culture. Some examples follow.

Dishonesty

The child learns from a parent "Do as I say, not as I do" when he is scolded for stealing even though Mom doesn't report the dog food under the cart in the grocery store. The same child may be reinforced in that dishonesty at school when a teacher asks for information about some misdeed, promising that the "honest" children won't be punished, then after the "naughty" children are turned in, the whole class loses privileges for a week. Children "taking care of" alcoholic parents learn that it is okay to lie to the boss about why your parents are not at work. Employees learn from a supervisor to mask or alter the facts when dealing with a sensitive situation "so people won't get upset."

Frozen Feelings

While "being nice" is one of the hallmarks of dishonesty, it paves the way to *frozen feelings*. Many church communities expect members of the congregation, especially women, to be nice to everyone. Those who do honestly express feelings or disagree with church policies are considered rude, difficult, heretical or un-Christian, or even immoral. For example, in a small college-town campus church, there was a young Vietnam veteran who had some problems. He sought out young women involved with church activities and wanted to be close to them. Some of the young women were afraid because of the gruesome stories he told about the prostitutes in Vietnam and because of his violent outbreaks of anger. The church leaders instructed the women to be nice to this troubled young man and to spend time with him. The women's personal safety and feelings of fear and danger were clearly secondary, and the women were encouraged to discount their feelings. The young vet's real needs, pain, and confusion were similarly discounted—all in favor of maintaining the "nice" public image of the community. All the young people involved were encouraged to be out of touch with their own feelings. Their feelings were frozen and their voices were silenced, so they did not rock the boat.

Those who do choose to express their feelings honestly, or to disagree, or to challenge a church policy are considered to be inappropriate or even immoral. People who get divorced, have emotional/mental illness, or show strong emotions in some way often experience shunning in their church congregation, just when they most need support. A church, like a family, can have a powerful "Don't rock the boat" rule, appreciating and expecting frozen feelings.

Thinking Disorders

Thinking disorders or confused thinking happen when you are in confused situations. When you are confused about what is happening in your environment because dishonesty is the norm, you may try to "figure it out." In *Co-dependency: Misunderstood—Mistreated*, Anne Wilson Schaef says that this is a subtle attempt to control the situation, and it is almost always ineffective. You get involved in obsessive thinking patterns because you believe that if only you can figure it out, everything will be all right.

Many school curriculums are set up to teach "subjects" but not the process of living. Students learn thinking disorders because they are taught not to trust their intuition or to synthesize the data they have from their lives. At times a child can learn more about life on the playground and in line waiting to go to music class than sitting in rows listening to the teacher talk about cursive writing. I recall a time in fourth grade when I was punished by being made to stand in a corner while others finished their penmanship activity. I had already learned how to write and was good at it. I had finished my assignment quickly and started to read a book quietly at my desk. I was punished for going too fast and for not following the teacher's pace. What did I learn? I learned to be dishonest, that no matter what I could do or what I knew, I should not stand out from the others. I learned that I should pretend to be average and not let teachers know what I already knew.

I learned to be secretive; it was us (students) against them (teachers). I learned that the rules were more important than new skills or independent learning; honest expression of my skills and pace was punishable. I learned in school that outside rules always override internal beliefs. While intuition and the ability to synthesize inner and outer messages are important for survival and health, I learned not to trust my own intuition or knowledge and that I should try to "figure it out." Thus I developed the *obsessive thinking* (thinking disorder) that I will be all right if only I can figure out what to do by following the outside rules. However, since outside rules can change or be imposed arbitrarily against our best interests, obsessive thinking can be never-ending, if we focus on the outside clues, rather than the clues and intuition we all have within.

Short-supply thinking is discussed by Melody Beattie in *Beyond Codependency*. You have been led to believe there is good stuff, like commitment, love, food, intimacy, sex, etc., out there, but there is not enough to go around. You may think that if you don't "grab all the gusto" you can right now, you won't get any. This thinking disorder causes you to become desperate, holding on tightly to what you have or scrambling to get a piece of something, whether what you have is good for you or not, just as Ed did when he dated a woman he didn't like so he wouldn't be alone. You may settle for less. You feel deprived even when you are not. Jerry grew up in a home where he could never be good enough to please his parents. He is now a successful businessperson making $100,000 per year. Yet he constantly questions his wife about her use of money when she buys groceries for the family. This short-supply thinking leads to obsessiveness , and it contributes to the co-dependent syndrome—the focus outside the self to cover the pain within.

Perfectionism

In school you learn that perfectionism is something to strive for: doing everything that your teachers tell you to do and getting all A's is the goal. This goal does not come without a price. For example, you may do everything the teachers say, at the price of not developing skills in decision making and analyzing. Even if you do get all A's, you may not be any happier or more self-assured—especially if you do not take the time to play with other kids and if you do not develop the social skills necessary to make and keep friends. You can get lonely very early in life. If you seriously competed for good grades, you may feel estranged and separate from others. And if you seriously worked hard for all A's and got B's and C's instead, you may have been labeled stupid or slow or been punished by your parents. Those B's and C's may have reflected difficulty in reading or taking tests. Grades in school may not reflect the keen, analytical, or creative mind. Einstein was not a straight-A student. Other children as competent as Albert Einstein may have internalized the failure message of lower-than-perfect grades and stopped trying to learn and grow.

Perfectionism is what competition is all about; it is about winning out over others and holding ourselves and each other to very high standards. The perfectionistic attitude separates us from each other, and we all feel the loneliness of that separation. The elusive feeling of superiority (which is the seductive part of the perfectionist trap) does not provide lasting pride or confidence in the long run.

I taught a gender role class in which students wrote a paper on their personal journey of gender identity—that is, how they came to be socialized as a male or a female. As the men described competitive games all the way back to grade school, they said that to win was everything and to lose was to be ashamed, to be worthless and valueless, to be a sissy (in other words, female). The women may have played competitive games at home, but in elementary school they were divided from the boys and encouraged to play more cooperative games—games that had no winners or losers, games like hopscotch. Yet they were devalued by the boys, who made fun of them as too frilly and soft, or stupid because they played silly games with no clear winners. Boys who win both academically and athletically are the best and most perfect. So if a boy is a recess or games winner, yet a C student, he still is not perfect even though he wins at recess games. However, boys are always better than girls because they are competitive. Yet girls are not even allowed to compete, so they occupy an inferior position regardless of their interests or skills. A girl could be a top scholar but still not be perfect because she is not physically competitive.

The men in my classes who are good athletes and win in college varsity sports are proud of themselves, and athletics provides them with an important identity. Yet while they feel superior on this level, they say that they lack skills in maintaining happy intimate relationships and feel inferior academically. The insecurity of the neglected or shamed parts of the self becomes very powerful and painful. The co-dependent person begins focusing more and more on something—anything—to keep that insecurity down.

5. Public Images of the Co-Dependent

The dysfunctional rules you learned in your family, school, and church, and in the world in general, live within you. They position themselves in your mind and heart. They lead you to feel unhappy, stuck, and co-dependent. Since you have lived with them so long, they feel comfortable and you don't notice them. They are real, however. Melody Beattie, in her book *Codependent No More*, says that "people don't make these rules. Addictions, secrets and other crazy systems make these rules to protect the addictions and secrets and keep the crazy systems in place. But people follow these rules. And people mindlessly pass them on from generation to generation. The rules are the guardians and protectors of the system—the crazy system." These rules bind co-dependent people together.

The outer, public image projected by some co-dependent people is often that of the responsible, loyal person who is in control and knows just what to do all the time. Such people project a persona of strength and security, yet underneath they have the opposite feelings of self-doubt, confusion, and insecurity. They often say, "Everyone thinks I am so strong. All my friends come to me with their problems. If they really knew what I am like, they would be very surprised and probably wouldn't even be my friends." To keep up this public image of strength, co-dependent people do the "appropriate" thing, gradually ignoring and denying their own feelings until they have a self-identity associated with a public image that keeps them lonely and isolated.

Super-Responsibility

"If I don't take care of things they just won't get done." Diane, a fifty-year-old secretary, expects herself to do all the work at family gatherings. Although she has several children who come with their spouses and children to holiday gatherings, she alone expects to do all the cooking and make all the necessary arrangements. Although others offer to bring food, she says, "No, I want this to be just so. I will take care of everything." Diane is afraid that the meal won't be perfect, with all the dishes complementary to each other and in matching bowls. Thus she takes responsibility for all the preparations. Diane generally does even more than she says she will, and others know they can count on her to go above and beyond to produce a great event. So others do nothing and expect Diane to do everything. It is too much of a struggle to help her. She will not participate in a cooperative effort because she believes it is her job to be super-responsible. When asked how her holiday was, she usually says tiredly, "It was a lot of work." Diane, by excluding her family from participating in holiday "work," keeps them away from her emotionally as well as out of the kitchen. Diane doesn't enjoy the work, and she is worried even if everything turns out all right—worried that the food was well cooked, done on time, and that everyone was happy. She doesn't know how she feels and consequently doesn't share that part of herself. Being super-responsible is her way of being useful, following the rules, and seeking appreciation. Her family may well be grateful, but her family's gratitude is never enough for her to feel okay about herself.

Self-Blame

"I should have planned for that." Denise, a lesbian, had been Nancy's partner for ten years. She prided herself on being very organized, and "Be prepared" was her motto. When Denise and Nancy went to visit Nancy's family for the weekend, they went on a picnic and hike at a nearby state park. While Denise, Nancy, and some other family members were hiking, Nancy tripped and cut her foot badly. Denise was immediately angry with herself because she had not brought a first-aid kit on the hike (naturally, she had one in the car). They did make it back to the car, and to the hospital where Nancy's cut was treated. She missed several days of work while her foot healed. For weeks, Denise worried about not bringing the first-aid kit on the hike. She kept saying that Nancy would not have had such a bad injury if she had only thought of this. She blamed herself for not thinking of everything. Denise's worry illustrates the illusion of responsibility a co-dependent person can have—and how the focus on and preoccupation with that responsibility distracts from other issues—like Nancy's basic responsibility for herself, and Denise's own inner life.

Pseudo-Fragility

"I don't know how much more of this I can take!" Peggy is always on the edge, it seems. On the edge of what, no one is quite sure. But she talks as if one more pressure or expectation will make her snap. So she has trained most people at work and in her family to expect very little from her. She always seems to be in some kind of crisis, and she looks tired and moves slowly. Others tiptoe around her, fearful that she may actually have a yelling fit directed at them. When she is late for work, her boss and colleagues do not mention it. When she does not do something she said she would do for one of her children, one of the other children takes care of it. She maintains a pseudo-fragile image. Her constant-crisis illusion keeps people away and prevents any honest communication. Peggy avoids responsibility, and keeps her environment stirred up and distracting. No one, least of all Peggy, knows what is really hurting her.

Many co-dependent people become addicted to compulsive spending, compulsive working, compulsive sexual activity, excessive drinking, or obsession with food (anorexia, bulimia, or constant eating). Stress-related physical problems, such as headaches, backaches, or gastrointestinal distress, are common too. These are the more obvious problems you are apt to see. Sometimes these obvious problems seem to disappear. The person who drinks too much, for example, may stop drinking, and the "problem" may appear to be solved. Headaches may be relieved with new drugs. But underneath the pain remains, and the desperation to avoid and deny it continues. For some co-dependent people, an image of powerlessness or sickness serves the same function as one of super-responsibility. Both are ways to focus or obsess outside the self.

Hypochondria

"I hardly get over one cold when I catch another." Jane was hired as a new staff person and her colleagues were thrilled because she had some new ideas and skills that would be valuable to the agency. However, it seemed that she was spending a lot of time away from work because either she and or one of her two teenagers was ill. She had many doctor's appointments, and she often had to pick up one of the teens at school. During the year she worked at the agency, her sick time was extended to the limit. She missed many meetings, and over the course of several months the rest of the staff began to feel they could not depend on her. There seemed to be a physical crisis in her family most of the time.

Hypochondria is an attitude of fearing sickness and consequently having sickness frequently. Jane's sickness was a way for her to avoid regular responsibilities and interactions with her colleagues. Since physical illness is a generally accepted way to take time off, people rarely question it until, as in Jane's case, the behavior is excessive over time.

Bernie Siegel in his book *Peace, Love and Healing* talks of the attitudes of people who are physically ill. When he asks them what is wrong, they may say, "Nothing." When you deny your feelings and needs, or act as though everything is fine when it is not, it is a "die" message for your body. Your body will do what it thinks your mind wants. He says your body will get sicker and die sooner.

Siegel offers suggestions on how to get sick:

1. Don't pay attention to your body. Eat plenty of junk food, drink too much, take drugs, have lots of unsafe sex with lots of different partners—and above all feel guilty about it. If you are over-stressed and tired, ignore it and keep pushing yourself.

2. Cultivate the experience of your life as meaningless and of little value.

3. Do the things you don't like and avoid doing what you really want. Follow everyone else's opinions and advice, while seeing yourself as miserable and "stuck."

4. Be resentful and hypercritical, especially towards yourself.

5. Fill your mind with dreadful pictures, then obsess over them. Worry most if not all of the time.

6. Avoid deep, lasting, intimate relationships.

7. Blame others for all your problems.

8. Do not express your feelings and views openly and honestly. Other people won't appreciate it. If at all possible, do not even know what your feelings are.

9. Shun anything that resembles a sense of humor. Life is no laughing matter.

10. Avoid making any changes which would bring you greater satisfaction and joy.

Siegel suggests that people need to break out of self-denial and punishment to become real and authentic, and to affirm themselves. This means facing the negative messages learned in childhood and making efforts to change them as an adult—to heal the child within.

Powerlessness

"I've tried everything to get him to stop working so much." When Shirley married Joe, she was impressed with how successful he was as a teacher. In fact, he had been voted a teacher's excellence award the past year. Joe spent many hours preparing for his classes—every weekday evening, all day Saturday, and Sunday evenings. Shirley wanted to spend more time with Joe and told him so, although she tried to understand his interest in his work. Joe said his goal was to be a good teacher and the preparation time was necessary. Shirley began to feel powerless more and more in the relationship and was tense and irritated a lot of the time because she couldn't get Joe's attention. Eventually she gave up trying to change Joe's behavior. She became depressed, she stayed home while he was at work, and she watched TV and felt lonely and unloved. Shirley hoped for the best, expected the worst, and never enjoyed the moment—a position of powerlessness. She did not think, or figure things out, or make decisions. She stopped knowing what she wanted or what was best for her.

Co-dependent people avoid looking honestly at their own actions, attitudes, or expectations, and avoid making changes in themselves. Their focus is on changing the other person or circumstance, or on feeling guilty, but not on changing themselves. Whether co-dependent people seem fragile and helpless or steady and powerful, they all are frightened, needy, vulnerable children who are aching and desperate to be loved and cared for.

6. Vulnerable Groups

Some particularly vulnerable groups often exhibit co-dependent patterns. Women are socialized to become nurturing and other-focused, and motherhood is a made-to-order job for co-dependent patterns. This is also true of the helping professional, who may be a counselor, nurse, social worker, clergyperson, or in any other job that requires attention to caring for people. If emotional boundaries are unclear, and helping and caring are the expectation, these groups are often vulnerable to co-dependent patterns.

Women

Women are generally socialized to be nurturing and caring for others. They are often expected to be the "social glue" in families and at work. Women play an important role in the care and feeding of relationships. They are socialized to support relationships with men, women, and children, and they may provide much of the support and nurturance needed in healthy relationships. This is a valuable role. Jean Baker Miller says, "Most women find a sense of value and effectiveness if they experience all of their life activity as arising from a context of relationships and as leading on into a greater sense of connection rather than a sense of separation."[1] She examines the kinds of connections that women experience. Miller says that a large part of a woman's life is spent in "the active participation in the development of other people," and that women use their powers to increase the powers of others,

---

1. Jean Baker Miller. *Toward a New Psychology of Women*, 2d edition (Boston: Beacon Press, 1988, p. 156.

that is, to increase others' resources and strengths in many dimensions, emotional and intellectual.

Women may instinctively know that mutual interest and attention in a relationship gives both people a feeling of power (or empowerment) to appreciate and act on their own feelings or "listen to their own inner voice." Miller says that as the "quality of the relationship grows, the individual grows. So the goal is not to increase a sense of separation but to enhance connection to others, and in turn, this connection leads to more growth."

All people learn about themselves in relationship to others, although women are expected to do so more than men. Most psychological theories, however, are based on the concept of maturity as becoming separate from others. So women have been taught that they are not psychologically healthy because they often define their lives in relationship to others, and men are taught that they are psychologically healthy because they define their lives in separation from others. Either extreme is unhealthy.

Women do not always get the nurturance, emotional support, and intimacy that they need from others. This can happen especially in relationships with men who were not taught to be nurturing and to show emotional caring. While socialized to help and nurture, women are not socialized to ask directly for what they want and need for emotional support.

Women are further socialized to care for and be responsible for others in the extreme. Women are expected to sacrifice for their families and loved ones. When this socialization is paired with the rules of an unhealthy family, school, or church (don't trust yourself, don't rock the boat), women lose their inner selves. While trying to find meaning in relationships and connections, the co-dependent woman can focus only on the wishes, needs, and problems of others. She has no connection to her inner self and world of feelings, all that being the pain and insecurity that is avoided and denied. There can be no healthy connection, no satisfying relationship for her. If you are not connected to your "own voice" (that is, do not know or listen to your own needs or feelings), you cannot make honest connections to others or expect them to know your "voice" or needs and feelings. Carol Gilligan's book, *In a Different Voice*, is a good resource for learning more about this idea.

Women who work are encouraged to be in fields that help others, are less leadership-oriented, and don't take too much time away from family responsibilities. Some argue that things are changing today. However, the major shift has been role increase, not role change. That is, a woman is expected not only to do what she has always done—clean, cook, raise children—but now in addition she is expected to help support the family financially and to fulfill her own needs for meaningful activities outside the home. This has increased her stress and decreased the amount of time she has to focus inside herself in order to become more self-aware. She experiences what Lerner calls "de-selfing" or giving up her self.

Women watch their mothers take a back seat to other family members in buying new clothes, eating last at the dinner table after everyone else is taken care of, doing all the household chores. Women's training is very much in how to be co-dependent—to focus on the needs of others to the exclusion of themselves. In the extreme, women can be chronically self-neglectful and become resentful and unhappy. Women often show their anger and hurt in indirect, other-focused ways. Since relationships are so important, controlling the relationship is a common way to express anger—through nagging, interrupting, over-protecting, talking for others, and being passive-aggressive (getting even, not mad).

In *Dance of Intimacy*, Lerner discusses underfunctioning and overfunctioning. *Underfunctioning* is avoiding responsibility for things in your life, feelings, business, initiative, allowing someone else to make your decisions for you. *Overfunctioning* is thinking of everything, taking responsibility for others' business, having it all taken care of. You will usually recognize that underfunctioners need to change, since they seem weak or pitiful. You don't often think that overfunctioners need to make changes in their lives because they seem to have everything under control. The key is that overfunctioners need underfunctioners—thus the unhealthy balance. Overfunctioners must find someone willing to give up control; underfunctioners must find someone to take care of them—they pair up. Women who overfunction emotionally try to maintain a position of control through the nurturing and over-protecting of others at home and work, and they usually take responsibility for the emotional life of their relationships. Women who underfunction "care" for their partners by passively allowing the partner to make all the decisions, speak for them, call the shots. An underfunctioning woman doesn't confront or challenge disrespect, unreasonable demands, or neglect—she sees her job as acquiescing in order to make life more peaceful, to give her partner some peace and quiet, to maintain the balance.

Those of you who are overfunctioners are often, but not always, the firstborn. You stepped in to take over responsibilities that a parent or sibling was unable to handle. You step in to be the fixer, mediator, the one who saves the day. Since overfunctioners look good, their needs and problems are often overlooked by themselves and others. When you hit the wall or have been functioning in high gear for too long, you may fall in an especially big way.

Some time ago, I was very busy teaching, counseling, and working as an administrator at a university. I was considering a job change, my family was going through a crisis, I was presenting programs at several conferences around the country, and a friend was talking to me about his suicidal feelings. I was trying to be the perfect partner, teacher, counselor, administrator, daughter, granddaughter, friend, presenter, and traveler. I experienced severe role-overload and entirely too much stress to remain stable and healthy. I got sicker than I had ever been in my life. I was so weak, I was forced (and I do mean forced) to lie down for three weeks. Illness and total exhaustion was about the only thing that could keep me from trying to take care of what I thought were my responsibilities. Since I was too sick to read, watch TV, talk, eat, or move very much, I slept and thought (with my eyes closed). After a stubborn week of insisting that I could accomplish everything, I finally figured out that I needed to make some big changes in my life. I was trying to do far too much. I needed to eliminate some things, to create a balance of rest and work. Also, I realized that I needed to discontinue my work as an administrator and do what I loved: therapy and teaching. I am now doing that, and I have not been ill since then.

Underfunctioners are often middle or youngest children in the family, accustomed to having others taking care of them. If you are an underfunctioner, you learned early to hide the strong or assertive parts of yourself and present the needy, helpless, or naive side for attention. You found that if you didn't feel able to cope with something, a sibling or parent (an overfunctioner perhaps) would step in and do it for you. The underfunctioners don't "look good" and end up with lots of attention, but the dynamic of avoiding the inner self is the same. Underfunctioners look to other people to make their decisions for them; they are out of touch with their feelings and dreams and aren't confident about what they need or what they want to do.

Rebecca is a twenty-eight-year-old graduate student. She looks young, and her personal style is both childlike and seductive. Her relationship history is full of men who were considerably older, usually unavailable for long-term commitment (often married), and emotionally vulnerable. Rebecca often chose someone who would take care of her financially, help with decisions about academics or the job search, and give her a place to live. Her partner would become dependent on taking care of her and on the sexual intimacy they shared. It wouldn't take long before Rebecca would become bored and angry with the relationship, find someone else, and leave. In therapy, she began to recognize her patterns and began to work on self-confidence and the strengths she had been discounting in herself. On her own, she decided to finish school and move to a city where jobs in her field were more available. She began to realize that showing only her naiveté and helplessness brought her relationships she didn't find satisfying in the long run.

Women (and people in general) do not necessarily over- or underfunction in all parts of their lives and relationships. A woman may be an overfunctioning mother and underfunctioning wife. Two people in a relationship may under- and overfunction in specific ways that just happen to mesh (one is obsessive about housework and neatness, one is a procrastinator and untidy). Each needs the other for the unhealthy balance. When one changes towards health, the whole system is shaken, and the other either changes for the better or leaves. Often overfunctioners are threatened, then amazed and delighted, when some incapacity prevents their usual super-responsible efficiency and the underfunctioners take over and do a great job. The underfunctioners are surprised and pleased as well to watch themselves taking care of business.

Helping Professionals

Helping professionals are trained to be empathetic and caring of others. Counselors, social workers, nurses, ministers and priests, and other helping professionals often have chosen these paths because of roles they learned in dysfunctional families. Helping professionals are especially encouraged and conditioned to ease the load for others and to take care of others' needs. Like most co-dependent people, they tend to be more focused on caring for others than for themselves, they work or live in high-stress environments, and they are often self-neglectful. Many are so busy helping everyone else, they are lonely. A significant proportion of the people in the helping professions are untreated adult children of alcoholics (ACOAs) and co-dependents themselves. Timmen Cermak found that 60 percent of a sample of counseling professionals in California were ACOAs. Many of the examples in this chapter focus on the counselor or therapist but any helping professional may find the issues relevant.

The co-dependent helping professional who is unable to define boundaries clearly and who is unfamiliar with treatment programs for addictive behaviors is unlikely to identify clients who are serving as enablers to addictive spouses, partners, or friends. You may not recognize the behavior of an enabling client as inappropriate even if it is maintaining a dynamic of chemical abuse, eating disorders, or other addictive pattern in another person. A priest who is aware that his parishioner's spouse is an abusive alcoholic may advise only patience, understanding, and prayer. That advice may keep the family in danger and allow the violence and cycle of pain and denial to escalate.

One counselor, Mona, said that when she first started as a counselor, she wanted to be in the pilot's seat. She wanted to pick the final destination of her clients and wanted to navigate the course. Mona believed that she should be able to heal, no matter how severely ill or resistant her court-appointed clients. It took several years for her to realize that she needed to be a co-pilot and that she must accept the client's pace. Clients grow by exploring their thoughts and feelings without the condemnation that comes with the therapist needing to be in control.

Need for Approval

Helping professionals who have co-dependent patterns may carry these patterns into their work in several ways. If you have an excessive need for approval and a high tolerance for inappropriate behavior, you may try to avoid conflict. You may not confront a hostile client who blames you for his or her problems. You may exhibit avoidance and denial by putting off inevitable conflicts with clients who need to consider treatment programs. You may tell yourself, "The client is not ready to hear the suggestion." This may be a decision based largely on your own need to avoid conflict. You may be too uncomfortable with your clients' disagreement or anger to attend honestly to their needs for treatment.

Honesty

If you and your client are both co-dependent people, neither of you may want to be honest. The development of trust occurs only if both client and professional are willing to say directly what their feelings are during the interaction. A co-dependent client may be unwilling to ask the helping professional for feedback or medical information for fear of a shallow or dishonest response. A co-dependent counselor may be unwilling to tell clients when he or she is angry about something.

Unclear Professional Boundaries

Counselors who have a difficult time separating their own need for friendship and control from the therapeutic needs of the clients may have difficulty setting limits for themselves and recognizing the clients' boundaries. One therapist arranged trades with her clients, rather than direct payment for sessions. At one time, the therapist had two clients, strangers to each other, refinish some woodwork in her house as payment for therapy. The therapist socialized with the clients-turned-refinishers, got her friendship needs met, and maintained control over the clients as she supervised the refinishing job. The refinishing took several days, much longer than the therapy sessions lasted, and the clients went away feeling used and angry. They felt as if they'd given more to the therapist than she'd given to them, and the therapist's attitude was that she was doing the clients a favor accepting the trade and being friendly. The lack of boundary clarity for the therapist became a hurtful situation for both the therapist and the clients.

Separation

The goal of most helping professions is to help others by encouraging them to find their own path, answers, and way of living. A co-dependent helping professional may delay termination of treatment when it is not in the best interest of the client to do so. If you are a professional who has some friendship needs, you may be unable to define a clear separation between yourself as a professional and the client. You may continue treatment with the client in order to maintain the relationship in response to your own needs. Helping professionals may get confused between how the relationship meets needs of their own and how they help the clients become more confident and independent.

Responsibility

If you as a helping professional confuse issues of responsibility, you may feel responsible *for* others instead of having the more internal focus of being responsible *to* yourself and *to* others. For example, you may feel responsible for providing answers, solutions, or details to clients. You may attempt to protect, control, or rescue clients, when more appropriate behavior would be to share perceptions with them. When asked by a client to make decisions or solve problems, a co-dependent professional will find it difficult to resist. No matter how brilliant your insights and strategies, the ability to change rests with the client.

I recently read a story about a counselor who was seeing a couple for marriage counseling.[2] During one session the wife complained that her husband did not help with the dishes. Although this was only one of numerous complaints each had regarding the other, the counselor chose to focus on it. In retrospect, he realizes that he had no plan as to where to go with the issue; he just believed strongly that men should help with housework. He also believed that people should invariably express their feelings. He therefore asked the husband to listen and encouraged the wife to share her feelings about the husband's not helping with the dishes. The more she voiced her anger, the more adamantly he refused to wash dishes. The more he refused, the more hurt and angry she became. The more she seemed hurt, the more the counselor questioned the husband about hurting her feelings. The counselor's increasing effort to change the husband's behavior met with his increasing resistance. The more the counselor encountered resistance, the more powerless and inadequate the counselor felt. The counselor attempted repeatedly to manipulate the husband to satisfy the wife in order to save himself from painful feelings. The counselor was greatly relieved when the session ended. He felt totally powerless to get the husband to change, and he concluded that he was inadequate as a counselor. He felt overwhelmed and sick to his stomach. It took some consultation with his supervisor to understand what happened. The counselor was trying to rescue the wife and realized later how disrespectful, manipulative, and controlling he was in believing that his clients could not resolve their own problems. He was pretentious enough to believe that somehow he could and should resolve their problems while the clients watched.

Humor

If you are a helping professional who takes life very seriously and is not easily spontaneous and playful, you may find it difficult to show a sense of humor with clients. Since humor is

---

2. Adapted from an article by Max H. Hines, "Whose Problem Is It?" *Journal of Counseling and Development* 67:2 (1988), p. 106.

often an important connection in relationships, this inability can be a disadvantage for you and your clients. During one therapy session, a client told her therapist that she was feeling suicidal and felt like jumping out the window of his office. The office was on the second floor. The therapist responded, "I don't think that would do the job." The client smiled, and they were then able to talk about the ambivalence of her feelings, and how the effect of an attempt was more interesting to her than actually ending her life.

Tolerance

If you have a high tolerance for inappropriate behavior by others, your clients may take advantage of that. A client may make abusive verbal attacks on you during treatment, call you several times a week for additional non-emergency help, not pay his or her bill, or chronically miss appointments. If you as a therapist respond to these behaviors with tolerance and acceptance, you will find yourself exhausted and angry all the time, and your clients will persist in their dysfunctional behaviors. When you set limits, have clear consequences for inappropriate behaviors, and express your own feelings, you maintain your own boundaries—a healthy personal response for self-care. Such behavior also helps clients understand that you, along with others, have personal limits or bottom lines that you will enforce for yourself. This will serve as a positive model for them as well.

Triangulation

In working with couples, the issue of *triangulation* can be a factor. If you are a co-dependent helping professional who has been a mediator in your own family, trying to patch up arguments between your mother and father, you may find yourself in the same position with couples who are clients. You may serve as an indirect link through which couples can communicate, while avoiding face-to-face talk about their feelings.

With one couple triangulation began after the third session. Each of them called me at home to get advice on dealing with an upcoming holiday weekend. Although we had talked about this in the session that week, they wanted to talk to me separately and wanted me to tell the other what to do, instead of communicating directly with each other. Resisting the pressure, I told each one to figure out what was best for themselves and to talk to the partner about it. You can become a mediator between couples who want to avoid direct communication with each other if you are unclear about your role as a helping professional.

7. How to Change

In *Dance of Intimacy*, Lerner states that "you can count on only two things that will never change. What will never change is the will to change and the fear of change. It is the will to change that motivates us to seek help. It is the fear of change that motivates us to resist the very help you seek." I experience this regularly as clients come to me for help in making their lives more fulfilling. Part of their resistance is evident when they want to know how to change others in their lives. Our strengths and weaknesses seem to be the same at times, and it is important to appreciate the positive and negative sides of your co-dependent patterns. The more you identify and appreciate the positive aspects, the more likely it is that you can change the negative aspects.

Because co-dependent patterns are learned, they can be unlearned. Behaviors can be changed so that life can be more satisfying and rewarding. You can transform the patterns you have learned. You can accept the gains and losses that come with taking charge of your life. Recovery from co-dependent patterns requires lifelong attention to the behavior you want to change. Change can be a constant and rewarding avenue, and there are some specific things you can do to make changes.

First you must accept and believe that it is okay to *change the rules*. It is okay to change your behavior and to have support in your recovery: in counseling, Al-Anon, support groups, or whatever. You may start out believing it is okay to break the rules, yet you must believe it is acceptable to change the rules.

The rules you learned as a child do not allow for the *self* to develop into a healthy, self-confident, and self-trusting person. If you change the rules, you can begin to regain the power to know, trust, and appreciate yourself. Some new rules suggested by Melody Beattie in *Beyond Codependency* are:

- It is okay to feel my feelings and talk about them when it is safe and appropriate, and I want to.

- I can think, make good decisions, and figure things out.
- I can have, talk about, and solve my problems.
- It is okay to be who I am.
- I can make mistakes, be imperfect, sometimes be weak, sometimes be not so good, sometimes be better, and occasionally be great.
- It is okay to be selfish sometimes, put myself first sometimes, and say what I want and need.
- It is okay to give to others, but it is okay to keep some for myself too.
- It is okay for me to take care of me. I can say no and set boundaries.
- It is okay to have fun, be silly sometimes and enjoy life.
- I can make good decisions about whom to trust. I can trust myself. I can trust a higher power.
- I can be appropriately vulnerable.
- I can be direct and honest.
- It is okay for me to be close to some people.
- I can grow and change, even if that means rocking a bunch of boats.
- I can love and be loved. I can love me, because I am lovable. I am good enough.

Although new ways do not feel comfortable at first, that is okay too. You can do it anyway. You can take charge of your changes and empower yourself to heal and become healthier. You must stick to the rules of honesty, approval, acceptance, empowerment, nurturing, and love.

You must *become an expert on yourself.* It is amazing that you may be an expert on anticipating others' behavior. You may know what they need or how they feel. Now, you may need to become re-connected to yourself. Earlier, I discussed the idea of disconnection: you do not listen to your own "voice," or you "de-self"; you become a stranger to your own needs and wishes. To change, you need to become an expert on your own feelings, needs, interests, and goals. If you want to state clearly what you want from others, or if you want to have an intimate relationship with another person, you need to know what you feel in order to share it.

A shift from the other-focus is particularly hard for over-functioners who truly believe that the other person will not survive without help. As you become more self-focused, relationships between you and significant others may not improve in the short run. New intimacy will not be evident in your relationships immediately. However, in the long run you will find that the other person in a relationship will become healthier as you do yourself. (She may also choose not to grow healthier. In that case she will attempt to get you to change back or she may leave to find someone who will allow her addiction and problems to continue.) It is a courageous act to change toward health and balance in a relationship because there are no guarantees of how the changes will affect the relationship. A healthy relationship has the best chance if you become self-focused and become an expert on yourself.

You begin by taking care of yourself. Self-care is an attitude toward yourself and your life that says, "I am responsible for myself. I am responsible for leading or not leading my life. I am responsible for tending to my emotional, physical, spiritual, and financial well-being. I am responsible for identifying and meeting my needs. I am responsible for solving my problems and for my own choices. I am responsible for what I give and receive and for setting and achieving my goals." It is an attitude of respect for yourself.

Moving Toward Undependence

You are not helpless, and you can handle whatever life brings your way. Being yourself and being responsible for yourself do not have to be painful and scary. You don't have to be overly dependent on the people around you. However, there is no easy or magical way to become undependent overnight. You can ask yourself:

What do I need to take care of myself?
and
What am I supposed to learn?

There are some ways you can begin to answer these questions. In her book *Codependent No More*, Melody Beattie makes several suggestions:

Finish up business from your childhood, as best you can.
Grieve. Get some perspective. Figure out how events from your childhood are affecting what you do now. You may need to

go through a grieving process that includes expressing anger. There are some suggestions later in this book about the grieving process and how to express appropriate anger. Betty told me about one way she was able to work through her anger about some childhood experiences. Her mother had tried to control the activities of all three children in the family. Betty learned to do what her mother told her, and never considered rocking the boat. In fact, now in her thirties, she could seldom identify her own feelings— she had "de-selfed." Although she had been a member of a group for adult children of alcoholics (ACOAs) and in individual therapy, she still felt stuck and could not express anger. Betty finally attended a five-day, co-dependency in-patient treatment program. There she did extensive experiential emotional activities with the two counselors and six other patients. She cried a lot during the first few days, then she used the soft foam bats provided in the program for hitting and expressing anger openly. She hit things with the bats, screamed, cried, and said what she wanted to say to her mother. After this experience she talked of feeling lighter, forgiving herself and her mother. She set herself free of old but stubborn anger that had previously been expressed in confusion and depression. She could now identify her feelings and express them more directly. Although Betty continues her struggle with getting in touch with her feelings, she has *let go* enough to get the process started.

If you regularly recall and think about certain times in your life, that may be a sign that there are specific unresolved issues about those times. If you remember your father saying or doing certain things to you, you may need to explore the meaning of those memories to you. You may need to re-experience and release certain past memories to be set free from them.

Nurture and cherish that frightened, vulnerable, needy child inside you.

The child may never completely disappear, no matter how self-sufficient you become. Stress may cause the child to cry out. Unprovided for, the child may come out and demand attention when you least expect it. Make friends with your child, listen to his or her needs, and nurture this child by being gentle and trying to provide security for the child in you. Try not to judge the child in you harshly.

When the child in you feels angry, listen to him or her, talk to someone you trust about the anger. See if there is anything you can do to help the child feel more secure and less frightened. Janet was a successful businessperson, and people in her community looked to her for advice, emotional support, and information. On the outside she appeared strong, confident, self-assured. When she was ending a painful break-up with her partner, she became very sad and scared, did not want to face people, and began to withdraw because she didn't want anyone to see her "in such a mess."

As a child of nine, Janet had lost both her parents, and she had quickly become more adult. She seldom played with other kids her age and was very serious about being self-sufficient. She had a lost and fearful child in her as an adult. When she realized this, she slowly began to talk to friends about her fears, and she found a therapist whom she trusted and with whom she was able to talk about her vulnerability for the first time. Janet even began to enjoy the child-likeness that she had abandoned early in life. She began to welcome this child into her life. She grew closer to her friends, who also welcomed this new side of her. This part of her very slowly became more secure and integrated into her character.

Stop looking for happiness through other people.

Your source of happiness and well-being is not inside others; it is inside you. Learn to center yourself inside. Look for approval, peace, and well-being within yourself. Ask yourself frequently: What would make me happy at this moment? Then do the thing that would make you happy. For years, Tom had known that he wanted to be a teacher, and he had a teaching degree. Although he was gregarious and liked being with people, he worked for his dad as an accountant for five years after he completed a master's degree in business. He was afraid that his father would be disappointed in him if he left the family accounting business. At one point, he became very depressed and withdrawn. He finally talked to a friend and his spouse about his dream of being a teacher. They encouraged him to tell his father and to pursue a teaching job. To his surprise he got a teaching position in a nearby school. So he stopped working for his dad and started teaching, and he felt free, energetic, healthy, and happy. As he pursued his love for teaching, his relationship with his father improved, because Tom was happy with himself. When he stopped allowing his father's happiness (or at least what he thought meant his father's happiness) to define his own happiness, Tom's enjoyment of life improved greatly.

You can learn to depend on yourself.

Maybe other people haven't been there for you, but you can start being there for yourself. Look into your own eyes in the mirror every day and say, "I am a good person, I like myself the way I am, and I deserve the best." Attend to your own needs, and trust your intuition to know that you have good judgment about what you need. Trust that you can solve your problems and cope with life events as they happen. You can ask others for support and encouragement, yet know that you are responsible for your own happiness. As you become more self-focused, you can have a more responsible position in a relationship. Rather than reacting to how the other person sees the relationship, you can have your own definition of the relationship. This requires some degree of emotional "separation" on your part.

Strive for undependency.

Begin examining the ways you are dependent, emotionally and financially, on the people around you. Feel your feelings, talk about your fears, accept your present situation. You may feel scared as you begin to make changes. Do what you know must be done. The power to transform your life comes from feeling your feelings, not ignoring them.

Irene came to therapy when she had been married to Dave for six years. She had two children, two and four years old. When I asked what she wanted out of therapy, she replied, "I want to save my marriage." She reported that the problems in the marriage stemmed from interference by Dave's father. She described Dave's talking to his parents every day of their honeymoon, and the father's calling Dave to come help him with a project whenever Dave was not working on a three-day shift. Dave would usually go, and often cancelled plans with Irene and the children. While Irene was critical of many things that Dave did, she blamed his father rather than him. When I asked her what she liked or loved about Dave, she did not say much. There was a great deal of anger between them. Irene expressed her anger by complaining; she told Dave that he needed to stay away from his father, that she would not allow him to take the kids near him because there was too much "rough talking," and that his father criticized Irene in front of the kids. Dave expressed his anger through withdrawal. He didn't talk but would leave the house and go to his father's house. He didn't participate in the care of the children and he worked overtime whenever possible. Irene perceived this as punishment. Irene and Dave did not depend on themselves or each other for honesty, acceptance, or a listening ear. They were very angry, yet were unwilling to tell each other directly. They did not know how to express their feelings or desires clearly. Irene blamed Dave's dad for all their problems and said that if only he would "butt out," everything might be all right. After being in therapy for a while, Irene became clearer about her anger at Dave. She was able to see that she had been unhappy for several years.

As Irene began to regain some confidence, she said, "I have not gotten what I wanted for six years. I am going to set some limits and make some requests." Even though she had had no outside job for four years, had no formal training, and was financially dependent on her husband, she realized she would be better able to meet her needs if she were not married to Dave. She had depended on him to make her life happy in the past and was now ready to depend more on herself. Now that she was beginning to understand her own needs, she decided to change herself. She made plans: she got a job and her own apartment, and she began seeing friends regularly. After many months of grieving and struggling with her weight, her work, two children, and Dave, Irene was happier and more self-sufficient. She had learned that she could make changes in her life and that others were not responsible for making her happy.

■ Activity

There are some things you can do to increase your self-care. One activity you can do often is to stop and ask yourself, What do I need to do right this minute to take care of myself? Do this as often as you need to, and do it at least once each day. Then give yourself what you need. It can be anything—take five minutes to close your eyes and just feel sad or happy, do T'ai Chi, take a short walk, ask for a hug, make a phone call to a friend, just take a few deep breaths. You can also discuss with others what you need from them. Make some agreements with the significant people in your life, about what they can do for you. I have made an agreement with a friend: When she asks me how I am, she is prepared to give me at least five minutes to answer the question truthfully.

Acceptance

It seems paradoxical that you cannot change until you accept yourself as you are, yet it is true. Acceptance brings a sense of peace to your life. It is often a turning point in change, and naturally it is easier said than done. If you are a co-dependent person, you must accept your co-dependent characteristics in order to change. Also, you must accept that you are powerless over other people's addictions or any other circumstance you may have tried to control. You *cannot* control how much your partner, daughter, friend eats or drinks. You have learned that you are supposed to do things to please others. Yet you cannot control how other people feel or think or what they do. You can be responsible only for your own feelings, thoughts, and actions. These are difficult things to accept.

At the same time, acceptance does not mean tolerance. You do not need to resign yourself to situations where you are miserable. You do not need to accept any sort of abusive situation. Acceptance does mean that you acknowledge the present situation, then evaluate the circumstances and consider what you want to do for your own well-being. You need to accept patterns as inherently likely to repeat and to stop pretending that the abuse and pain will someday magically end.

If you learned to tolerate parents who yelled at you daily when you were a child, you may have learned that yelling is an acceptable, expected part of relationships. You may have chosen a partner who consistently yells obscenities and hurtful words at you. The yelling will not stop unless you do something different. You must accept that you are being yelled at, that you want it to stop, that it is abusive and inappropriate, then you must do something so you do not experience the yelling. Given that you can control only your own behavior, you can focus on what you need to change about yourself. You can tell your partner that you will not continue to listen to the yelling, that you will leave. And you *can* leave temporarily or permanently if the abuse does not stop.

The Grieving Process

As you make changes—starting to let go, setting boundaries—you begin your recovery. In your recovery, you will find yourself going through some particular stages of grief. Recovery is a healing process that involves giving up some old ways, having new awareness, and learning forgiveness. It is a powerful process of change and grief, and you will mourn what you lost and what you never had.

In her book *Death and Dying*, Elisabeth Kubler-Ross describes five stages of grief. Although Kubler-Ross is talking about grief for a physical death, grieving for an old self can be similar and very traumatic for you. Although new behaviors may be healthier, you go through an adjustment process, or grieving, when you make changes in your behavior that affect your entire life. For example, you may change the group of friends with whom you spend time. This means that you are saying good-bye to old friends while making new ones may take some time.

Kubler-Ross's stages of grief include the following:

Denial and Isolation. This is a state of shock, disbelief, and numbness about the loss. You may say "It just can't be," or "Things will be all right." You may find yourself doing things to avoid reality—sleeping a lot or keeping very busy. Denial acts as a buffer from unexpected shocking news. When my friends first told me I needed to deal with my own life and feelings rather than try to figure out what was wrong with the person who was leaving me, I said, "What do you mean? I am fine." To prove it, for a long time I stayed so busy that I did not have time to think about it. I did not want to accept the loss of my self-image as a picture-perfect healthy individual with no real problems.

Anger. This anger may be rational or not, and you may be furious with someone else or yourself. This can be a violent time for some, and professional help is recommended. It is a time when you are resistant to change, and still do not want to accept your loss. A friend of mine lost her mother to cancer, and she remained angry about her mother's death for several years. Whenever someone complained about his or her own mother, she would say angrily, "At least you have a mother." She was angry at God for taking her mother, angry that other people still have mothers, angry that it was not fair, angry that she had no more chances to make things right with her mother. A recovering co-dependent person may be angry at becoming aware that his parents did not give him the care he needed as a child and angry that there is no way to go back and get that care.

Bargaining. You may try to make a deal with a higher power: "If you bring him back, I will be a better friend," or "If she comes back to me, I will listen to her more." You may try to enter into some kind of agreement to postpone the inevitable. This is a time when you may try to get a lost love to return to you. You may say you will change or do whatever he wants if only he will come back to you. In a breakup or divorce, this is a time to be cautious. You may need to resist an invitation to renew an unhealthy or dysfunctional relationship.

Depression. Once you realize that the bargaining, the anger, and the denial have not worked, then sadness sets in, and the true mourning begins. This a time to cry and feel the hurt. You may be withdrawn, or cry a lot. You may not want to talk to people. You may sleep a lot, or not much. You may eat a lot, or not much. It is another important time to seek professional help, especially if others around you are saying, "You should be over this by now." You need someone who will listen to your hurt. You need to experience the hurt, acknowledge it, and move on. When you have worked through this process, you can move on to the final stage.

Acceptance. The anger and depression passes, and this stage comes with a sense of freedom and peace. You may feel comfortable dating or socializing or just staying home alone. You will feel you have in some way benefited from the loss—grown and been transformed to a new stage of self-acceptance. You may feel comfortable seeing or talking to the lost love, spouse, or parent. You may enjoy new or old activities with other people or alone.

■ Activity

To become more aware of yourself during the grieving process, set aside some time to look back over your life. Consider your losses. Consider the losses you feel in the present as you begin to acknowledge your co-dependent behaviors. Recall your experiences as they fit with what you know about the grief process. Write about your feelings.

Self-esteem

Your low self-esteem is tied into all aspects of your co-dependency, which may include workaholism, chemical dependency, refusal to enjoy life, martyrdom, perfectionism, rescuing, controlling, preventing intimacy, shame, staying in destructive relationships, avoiding people who are good for you, guilt, not allowing yourself to enjoy fully anything you do, and procrastination.

You must be willing to stop picking on yourself, to forgive yourself and to put your guilt aside. Co-dependents learn to disguise their true feelings about themselves by dressing right, working in a prestigious job, or living in the right home. Even though you look successful on the outside, inside you may feel that you will never be enough. You may feel guilty about not helping enough. When you have two choices, and you make one, you may think, "I should have made the other choice." You can punish yourself incessantly. You may even invite others to abuse you by allowing them to take advantage of you. You can have piles of "shoulds" which remind you of all the things that you *should* have done differently and all the things you *must* do in the future.

You must be willing to forgive yourself, recognize what your "shoulds" are, put these "shoulds" in a shoebox, put the lid on the box, put the box on the highest shelf in your closet, and leave it there. Do not let your "shoulds" interfere with the joy of your accomplishments, comforts, or loves. One difference between co-dependent people and others is that the rest of the people in the world don't pick on themselves for being who they are. Everyone has similar thoughts and feelings. All people make mistakes. You need to leave yourself alone about them.

If perfectionism is a problem for you, nothing you do seems good enough. Sure, things can always be improved, yet the obsession with making your job, partner, or child perfect will destroy any appreciation you can have for yourself and your life. Patience and taking time out just to pay attention to your inner self is especially important in order to appreciate the glory of each moment, rather than to focus on the unattainable perfect finished product.

You can be good to yourself, have compassion and kind-ness for yourself as you might for someone else you love. You can stop blaming yourself and give yourself positive messages—"I did a good job today." Guilt and shame and the "should" statements that go with them are useless and damaging to you and your enjoyment of life. You may catch yourself saying, "I should have helped my friends more," or "I should have known she was sick." Nothing you can do will change the past. Focusing on it is just one more way to avoid dealing with yourself in the present.

Messages of guilt and blame are largely a habit you have learned. You can unlearn them and begin to form new habits. When you begin to recognize that you are giving yourself "should" messages, force yourself to stop, think of something positive you have done or felt, and tell yourself about that. Or deal directly with your feelings and go ahead and feel them: "I feel vulnerable and inadequate now, and afraid no one will love me. I can love myself and take care of myself and get through this."

Boundaries

Co-dependent people do not know where they end and someone else begins. This is an especially important characteristic, and some feel it is the core of co-dependency. You may take on another's feelings, responsibilities, or opinions. Anne Wilson Schaef, in *Co-dependency: Misunderstood—Mistreated*, discusses the idea of being *externally referent*. You may get confused when others get confused, or you may jump in to rescue them from their confusion by telling them what they need to do to solve their problem. You are the "fix-it" person who can help them with whatever is the matter. You may feel fused to someone, or you may feel swallowed by another. You may hear yourself speaking of what I call the "Royal We." You speak for a group, not yourself or the "I." For example, you may say, "We feel tired today," when you mean that your child is feeling tired.

When you find yourself doing this, you need to feel your own feelings. Take a time-out; do not commit yourself to an activity that will rescue the other person. If you are confused, try to focus your attention inside yourself to see what you are feeling. No one else is ultimately responsible for your feelings, no matter how much you insist that they are. The statement "You are making me feel guilty" is simply not true. You feel guilty because of your own interpretation and view of the situation. No one outside of you can control your feelings.

If you learned that sacrifice is love, you may find yourself miserable and lonely. You don't have to be willing to lose everything for love. In fact, setting and sticking to reasonable, healthy limits or boundaries in all your relationships is necessary to love and relationships that work. You can make appropriate decisions about what you are willing to give and take in your relationships. Boundaries of your own simplify life. They do not complicate life. You no longer have to guess about someone else's needs. You can decide what you will do and stick to it.

A boundary is a limit that marks your personal territory or your self. This can be your body, your mind, your emotions, spirit, or rights. Although the boundaries may be invisible, they are real. Co-dependent people often team up with controlling people, or are over-controlling people themselves. Controlling people invade territory. They may think they have a right and even an obligation to do so. For you to get well and stay healthy, you need to set a limit so that other people do not invade your body, mind, or spirit and so that you do not invade someone else's body, mind, or spirit. Melody Beattie says in *Codependent No More*, "Without boundaries, relationships will cause us fear. We're vulnerable to losing all we have, including ourselves."

■ **Activity**

To practice achieving your inner focus and the awareness of boundaries, keep a regular log or journal in which you write observations about your feelings and activities. It should be guilt-free and private. Make sure that no one reads it. You may re-read it periodically to review which emotions come peeking out and which come roaring out. Try to recognize the circumstances and feelings of invasion of boundaries. When do you feel crowded, trapped? When are you aware of your limits and others' limits?

Find a person in your life who is honest, a good listener and a non-rescuer, and talk to him or her openly and honestly about your feelings. Listen to this person without judgment or caring gestures. How does this feel? If you do not have such a person in your life, join or start a support group. Also complete the Rescuer Checklist in the Appendix to see how much you try to serve as a rescuer. Then you can pay attention to some of the behaviors in this checklist. When you find yourself doing any of these things, make a note about it in your journal.

Anger

Co-dependent people often find it very difficult to express anger openly and honestly. When you begin to become more immediately aware of your feelings, there may be more anger than you care ever to feel. Yet, there it is, and it needs to be expressed and dealt with in some way. You may have been more aware of fear, sadness, and hurt than anger. In response you may be more likely to get even than to get mad. Yet anger and hostility are usually just below the surface, and anger can be seen in gestures or looks.

When you do need to express anger, it is difficult to know how to do it appropriately. Co-dependent people are often rather self-righteous, and they get angry at their partner when he or she gets mad. You may hear yourself saying, "After all I have done for you, how dare you be mad at me." Then later, you feel guilty and your self-worth becomes lower as you chastise yourself for losing control.

Lerner discusses anger gone wrong for women in her book *Dance of Anger*. There are two categories of anger, that of the "nice lady," who attempts to avoid anger and conflict at all costs, and that of the "bitchy woman," who gets angry with ease but participates in ineffective fighting, complaining, and blaming that leads to non-constructive resolution. Both types of anger serve to blur any clarity of self and ensure that change does not occur.

"Nice Ladies"

"Nice ladies" may stay silent or become tearful, self-critical, or "hurt." If you do feel angry, you keep it to yourself to avoid open conflict. This silence allows you to avoid making clear statements about what you think and feel, especially when you suspect that such clarity would make another person uncomfortable or you would expose the differences between yourself and others.

By preserving harmony at all costs, you are unable to achieve clarity about your needs or preferences. You can spend so much time "reading" others and ensuring you don't rock the boat that you become less and less knowledgeable about your own thoughts, feelings, and wants. You may develop a storehouse of unconscious anger.

"Bitchy Women"

The "bitchy woman" is seen as nagging and complaining. Although this characterization is part of a cruel sexist stereotype (women are *not* supposed to express anger in our society), it still implies helplessness and powerlessness. The woman feels "stuck," as if nothing will change. Although she may have something to be angry about, her complaints are not clearly voiced and she will elicit others' disapproval rather than sympathy. She may become more bitter and angry.

It takes a certain amount of courage to know when we are angry, and to let others know about it. When you don't have that courage, anger, blaming, and fighting make for an ineffective pattern. The pattern perpetuates itself. Others can write off an angry woman who seems to have no direct purpose or request.

The ineffective pattern gets others off the hook, and no one needs to be willing to change. When you fight ineffectively, you are usually trying to change another person who does not want to change. As the other person resists change, you get angrier and try to change his attitudes, actions, or feelings, and both of you are caught in a vicious cycle or spiral that escalates the problem. Thus the "bitchy woman" is as self-defeating as the "nice lady" and the problems are self-perpetuating. Both are left feeling helpless and powerless. As Lerner says, we "do not feel in control of the quality and direction of our lives."

Trash Compactor

I call the storehouse of anger your "trash compactor." Whenever you come across a feeling or thought you do not want to deal with directly, you put it in your personal trash compactor—your storage for hiding your thoughts and feelings from yourself and others. If you get "upset" or "irritated" by someone, you may say, "I don't want to hurt his feelings." Then you put this feeling in your trash compactor, close it, and mash it down with your other unfinished business. When you "hide" and try to "stuff" what you believe are "inappropriate" feelings, they come out sideways anyway. You may find yourself smiling while slamming kitchen cabinets.

Trash compactors get filled up at some point. The seams may begin to split or the motor may begin to whine and moan when you try to crush more trash. It is time to take the trash out. Your personal "trash compactor" gets filled too. Your "cup runneth over," and usually with anger. You may have a "tolerance break." When my trash compactor is filled and I have a tolerance break, my usual calm and kind nature vanishes, and I may become demanding, yelling about something that has caused me to lose my cool. Very soon after, I am embarrassed and apologetic about my outburst. The feelings from the outburst had little to do with what was going on at the moment. It just happened to be the last thing I tried to stuff in my trash compactor. During a tolerance break, the "nice lady" can become a raging woman. This is frightening to her and to others around her. It will probably be a surprise that knocks you for a loop.

Dorothy, who lived in the rural South, once told me about a woman who lived down the road from her. She said this woman "went plum haywire." At the time I didn't understand what happened to this woman, who had six children, many dogs, cats, and goats, an unruly mule, a nearly absent husband, and no regular income. As I look back on this, I see that she tried her best to be nice to everyone, to take care of her children, yet she had a huge "trash compactor" full of anger. When the seams broke open it was full of many years of bitterness, hurt, and anger about her feelings of powerlessness over her own life. As she tried to provide food and shelter for her children, she was eventually worn down and filled with anger. The "nice lady" was unable to store any more anger. All the frozen feelings she had stored all those years to keep the peace exploded all over the place.

Some ways of expressing anger are more constructive than others. Here are some suggestions from Melody Beattie's book *Codependent No More*:

Feel the emotion.

Anger produces emotional energy like any other emotion. It is just as valid as any other emotion you feel. If it is there, feel it. When I get mad, I need to move. I can feel the energy coursing through me, and it feels like it is going to burst out. My heart beats harder and I breathe faster. Once when I was on a car trip with a friend, I got very angry with him for some reason. (Naturally I cannot remember the context of the anger.) I stopped the car on the highway, got out, and started to walk. I probably could have broken some 100-yard dash records at that moment. I could feel the adrenaline coursing through my body. Slowly the physical energy subsided and I could think more clearly. I walked back to the car and got in, and I could then talk about what happened.

Look at the thinking that goes with the emotion.

Consider what the thoughts are that go along with your anger. See if there are any patterns or repetitions that you recognize. Often when I get angry, it has to do with someone doing something that slows me down from my usual fast pace. I am usually on a tight schedule (one that I created, mind you). So when I drive, I clip along and am often slowed down by someone going the speed limit. When I find myself getting irritated by the slowed pace, I ask myself why I am angry about slowing down. Usually, I find that slowing down means that I may not get somewhere on time or that I will not get done everything that I planned to do. So the thinking that I challenge is whether I must finish everything on my list during the time frame I have created. To get free of the anger, I try to change the thinking that created the list that controls my life. After all, I made the list, so I can change the list.

Make a responsible decision about what action, if any, you want to take.

Figure out what the anger is telling you. Do you have some unmet needs? Are there some things going on in your environment that you need to change? You may need to tell someone what you need from him or her. You can ask yourself, Am I afraid of being left out? Am I afraid to do something by myself? Sometimes you may get mad at a friend who is late and did not call to tell you of her late arrival. If you get mad at her, ask yourself what the anger is about. Are you scared when you think you may have lost her in a car accident, or that she is insulting you by not taking your feelings into consideration? Once you know what is behind these feelings, you can ask her for what you want to help you cope with these feelings.

Don't let anger control you.

You do not need to continue to scream. Screaming may help. Sometimes other things are needed as well. You may need a time-out, so go to a peaceful place away from the object of your anger and think about what you want. When Connie gets angry, she talks, cries, and screams, and the longer she does this, the more wound up she gets. She begins to think everything in the world is bad ("catastrophizing") and starts to blame the person she is with for all the problems she sees in her life. She lets her anger control her, and she does not take a time-out to consider what she wants and needs from others. She could take deep breaths, go to another room, go for a short walk, or do anything else that would break the downward spiral.

Discuss your anger openly and honestly when it is appropriate.

Be aware of how you approach people, and do not try to talk to a drunk, angry, or tired person. Pick the time and place so the other person will be most likely to listen. Molly stays home with the children; by the end of the day she is tired and angry, and she begins to think that her husband is not helping care for the children enough. When he comes home from work at 6:00 P.M., Molly meets him at the door, complaining that he doesn't do enough to help her at home and asking that he start to help right now. He too has had a stressful day of work and does not respond kindly to this attack at the front door. Molly could ask if they can talk later, after everyone has eaten, read the mail, relaxed for a while. Picking your time can make a big difference in the presentation and the response.

Take responsibility for your anger.

You are angry. He did not make you angry. What he did may have been the catalyst, and then you responded, and you are responsible for that response. I often hear people say, "He made me angry because he would not do what I told him." I realize this is an acceptable cause-and-effect statement for most. I believe, however, that whatever responses or feelings you have are a result of your own interpretation and experience in life. No one can make you feel anything. I believe that when people say, "You made me do it, lose control," they are saying, "I do not want to take responsibility for my own response and feelings."

Burn off the anger energy.

Do whatever you like to use the energy in an activity—wash the car, jog, clean a closet, turn the music up loud and dance. It helps to discharge the energy physically. I often go for a walk to get away from the object of my anger, to burn off the physical energy, and to allow my body to return to a regular rate of heartbeat so I can think more clearly about the situation.

Do not hit when feeling angry.

Do not allow yourself to hit, or others to abuse you, during angry feelings. If abuse has occurred, seek professional help. Because the physical energy of anger can be strong, hitting and throwing things is commonplace. Men especially are taught to express their feelings physically. However, striking another person to express anger is an unacceptable way to burn off the energy.

Write letters you do not send.

Write out your feelings to those with whom you are angry. You can discharge a lot of negative energy by writing down your resentments. This is especially helpful to bypass guilt and get to the point of being clearer about what you want from the other person. Martha went through a difficult breakup, with her partner a few years ago. She was very hurt and angry with him, yet he had been her best friend and lover for several years, and she did not want to alienate him. For the first month of the breakup she wrote letters to him in a notebook. She did not send these letters, but kept writing him. Two things happened. She became clearer about how she felt about him and the situation. And she was able to talk to him about her concerns without feeling so angry that she was out of control. In this way she was able to communicate more clearly, be aware of her feelings, and not alienate the other person.

Get rid of the guilt.

Do not hold on to your guilt. Throw it all away. It does not help and can create continued problems as you allow yourself to stay stuck in a situation where you feel like a victim. As suggested earlier, whenever you feel guilt, imagine that you put your guilt in a shoebox, put the lid on the box, put the box in the closet, and close the door. Whenever you feel guilty later, imagine doing this again.

■ Activity

Write down how the people in your current living situation deal with anger. Write how your mother, father, and any siblings deal or dealt with anger. Write how you deal with anger now. If anger is a troublesome feeling for you, keep pencil and paper with you all the time. As soon as you feel anger, write about your anger as it happens.

Intimacy

In her book *Codependent No More*, Melody Beattie discusses self-defeating patterns of intimacy and intimacy avoidance. You may keep having the same problems in relationships over and over. You may feel that people keep doing the same things to you. You need to look at how your present relationships connect to your past relationships.

Co-dependent people get confused between being needed and being loved, and are attracted to someone who they believe needs them. They choose partners who are needy—an alcoholic, an emotionally unavailable person, someone who is depressed and unable to keep a job. You may stay with him even when he has little to offer in meeting your needs. And for awhile being needed is enough, even if you can't count on him to care for you or to do as he says.

When you find yourself thinking and talking about nothing but one person, you are obsessed with this person. You have allowed this person to control you—this person has top priority for you. You have allowed the obsession to interfere with the other parts of your life. Worrying and obsessing keeps you so tangled in your head that you cannot solve your own problems. When you are attached to someone in this way, you are detached from yourself. You have forfeited your power and ability to think, feel, act, and take care of yourself. You have *de-selfed*.

Intimacy is often confused with sexual activity. Intimacy may include sex, yet it is much more than sex. In *Dance of Intimacy*, Harrriet Goldhor Lerner says that "intimacy means that you can be who you are in a relationship, and allow the other person to do the same. 'Being who you are' requires that you can talk openly about things that are important to you, that you take a clear position on where you stand on important emotional issues, and that you clarify the limits of what is acceptable and tolerable to you in a relationship. Allowing the other person to do the same means that you can stay emotionally connected to the other person who thinks, feels, and believes differently, without needing to change, convince, or fix the other.

The good news is that you learn this kind of intimacy. You need to "detach." Detaching is difficult at first, yet ultimately it works better for everyone involved. Detaching means "mentally, emotionally and sometimes physically disengaging yourself from unhealthy entanglements with another person's life and responsibilities, and from problems you cannot solve," according to a handout entitled "Detachment" distributed by Al-Anon. It means keeping your hands out of other people's business. You are each responsible for your own actions, feelings, and thoughts. You need to pay attention to your own and not another's actions. You need to decrease your obsession with others' thoughts, feelings, and actions and maintain a focus on your own thoughts, feelings, and actions.

Detachment is also "present-moment living"—being in the "here and now" and not trying to control the situation. Accept the situation as it is—respect the natural order of things. You can trust that all is well in spite of conflicts. You can be involved, love and care about another without feeling out of control, without feeling responsible for them. Melody Beattie, in *Codependent No More*, says that detachment is both an act and an art. It can become a habitual response. You can detach with love, even though you may feel angry. Once you detach from someone whom you used to think, talk, and worry about much of the time, there is room to take care of yourself.

Change in relationships is a constant—they are cyclical not stable. There are cycles of struggle, closeness, passion, boredom, distance, joy, pain, and growth. If you are willing to learn to be intimate in a relationship, you must also be willing to accept the cycles and work through them. This requires flexibility and honesty of both partners.

■ **Activity**

If there is a person in your life whom you are excessively attached to or worried about, write about that person or problem. Write as much as you can. Then when you have written as much as you can, focus on yourself. Write how you feel and what you think. How do you feel about detaching from that person? What will happen if you detach? What will happen if you don't detach? How has staying "attached"—worrying, obsessing, trying to control—helped so far? If this person were not in your life, what would you be doing today, this week? Spend some time visualizing your life without this person.

Transforming to Undependence

If you are living your life for another, your parents, lover, employer, then you are saying, "I am not good enough," and that builds self-hatred and denial. Saying "I come first" is taking care of yourself. It is not selfish. It is an act of loving yourself. You are your own parent now, and you can take charge. You can transform your life and become powerful, able to live joyously.

There are many gains and losses as you focus inward rather than outward for answers. You discover new ways of feeling, acting, and living more freely and comfortably with yourself and others. With new freedom to express long-repressed feelings comes the responsibility and fear of owning them. If you are honest with yourself, it is a struggle to maintain comfort in an addictive society. Most people work in institutions that expect you to follow the rules even if they are hurtful to someone. Church members are expected to accept church doctrine even if they do not agree or even if it does exclude certain minority groups. As you feel and express your feelings and thoughts more honestly, you will find yourself in more battles with the systems where you live and work.

Parents of physically and emotionally disabled children talk of the changes in their personal struggles and the expressions of them, after their disabled child was born. Penny said that she used to be a quiet, passive person who accepted the word of teachers, doctors, and other helping professionals. Now Penny says, "I feel like I am fighting with professionals all the time. Just to get the services that my child deserves, I must argue with school systems that are not prepared to teach my child. I must demand that I be involved in the process of medical decisions to treat my child in the hospital." This transformation happened as she was forced to deal with the reality of her special-needs child.

In some ways we all have special needs, and we are forced to deal with school or medical systems or with work situations that are not built to attend to those special needs. We are encouraged to keep quiet, to fit in, to follow the rules. If you do "rock the boat" when your supervisor wants you to be a team player, you are branded as a troublemaker. Thus, one of the primary losses of becoming more self-focused and more expressive of your needs is the loss of the anonymity that you may have found very comfortable. You may now feel more conflicts with other individuals or systems—"no more Mr./Ms. Nice Person." Niceness and dishonesty can be very similar, and if you thought of yourself as nice and even prided yourself on being nice, you may lose that identity as you become more honest with yourself and others. As you gain a greater sense of your new identity, you lose and may grieve for the days when life seemed easier, the days of innocence when you did not know what you wanted. Remember that those days were also filled with confusion, frustration, and depression.

How Recovery Starts

The Recovery Checklist in the Appendix can help you identify your strengths and weaknesses in your recovery. You may also use it to set goals for your recovery. It can also help you understand how you can start your recovery.

Clarity about the need for the change often occurs when you have an interruption in your life. This can be an illness, a death, the birth of a child, a change in job responsibilities, a vacation, a meeting with someone who turns your head, or a divorce—or any other expected or unexpected change. It happens when you have time to think about things or you are forced to reevaluate the way you go about living your life. Once this process starts, you may begin to reevaluate many aspects of your life. You may wonder if you have ever in your life been awake. John and Linda Friel say in their book *Adult Children* that

> regardless of our symptoms or circumstance, we are Adult Children of dysfunctional families because: something happened to us a long time ago. It happened more than once. It hurt us. We protected ourselves the only way we knew how. We are still protecting ourselves. It isn't working anymore.

You may begin to change when you recognize the need for it. This happened to me when I got very sick a few years back. I was forced to stop my routines and my marathon of activities. My life was interrupted and the time came when the message was clear—something was amiss in my life. That is when change started for me. I started the necessary soul searching to figure out how to make my life more meaningful. I thought about what makes me feel good—what work, which people, what recreational activities. Change started when I asked the questions and I looked *inside* for the answers. I realized I could trade the illusion of control for true control by facing myself squarely and doing what I knew was best and by sharing honestly with others what I found inside.

What Positive Change Feels Like

Changing, bringing your self to life, takes consistent and persistent attention on your part. You have learned to be the way you are through many years of training and socialization. You have been encouraged to be like others, not to rock the boat. Changing is a struggle that means paying attention to what you do, feel, and say. It means that others will resist your changing because they were used to you the way you were. It is up to you to make changes and to find a support system for your new self. If you decide to do this, you will reap some powerful benefits.

Positive change will bring you some new feelings about life. Some of these may be:

- You feel new potential: there is hope.

- Life is exciting; the future is interesting, not frightening.
- When you express anger, you feel free to look to the future with hope and interest.
- You begin to breathe freely.
- You recognize the unmanageable parts of life and let them go.
- You affirm yourself every day; when life feels difficult, you start affirmations to rebuild your self-worth.
- You feel worthy and proud of yourself; you validate yourself.

These feelings will come at different rates, some slowly and some right away. Patience is especially important as you make changes. It has taken you a number of years to learn the patterns you are familiar with, and it will take some adjustment and practice as you make positive change, as you bring your self to life.

Appendix

Recovery Checklist

___ Maintain appropriate daily routine

___ Setting and achieving daily and long-term goals

___ Personal care

___ Setting and sticking to limits with children and others

___ Constructive planning

___ Appropriate decision-making and problem-solving efforts

___ Choosing behaviors

___ Well-rested

___ Resentment-free

___ Accepting (versus denying)

___ Not controlling others or feeling controlled by them

___ Open to appropriate criticism and feedback

___ Free of excessive criticism of self and others

___ Gratitude versus self-pity and deprivation

___ Responsible financial decisions (not over- or underspending)

___ Appropriate nutrition (not over- or undereating)

___ Not escaping or avoiding through work or sex

___ Self-responsibility (versus scapegoating and blaming)

___ Valuing wants and needs

___ Free of victim self-image

___ Free of fear and anxiety

___ Free of guilt and shame

___ Free of worry and obsession

___ Not feeling excessively responsible for others

___ Faith in Higher Power

___ Trusting and valuing self

___ Making appropriate decisions about trusting others

___ Maintaining recovery routine (attending support groups, etc.)

___ Mind clear and peaceful; logical thinking; free of confusion

___ Feeling and dealing appropriately with feelings, including anger

___ Appropriately disclosing

___ Reasonable expectations of self and others

___ Needing people versus NEEDING them

___ Feeling secure with self; self-affirming

___ Communicating clearly, directly, and honestly

___ Balance mood

___ Maintaining contact with friends

___ Feeling connected and close to people versus lonely and isolated

___ Healthy perspective; life looks worth living

___ Not using alcohol and medication to cope

___ Having fun, relaxing during leisure activities, enjoying daily
     routine

___ Giving appropriate positive feedback to self and others

___ Getting—and allowing self to believe—positive feedback[1]

---

1. From Melody Beattie, *Beyond Codependency and Getting Better All the Time*, pp. 73-
74, and based in part on "Relapse Warning, Signs for Co-Alcoholism," developed
by Terence T. Gorski and Merlene Miller, for "Co-Alcoholic Relapse," in *Co-dependency, An Emerging Issue* (Hollywood, FL: Health Communications Inc. 1984, p.82)

Rescuers Checklist

Completing this checklist can help you become aware of ways you may be rescuing people without realizing it. It is published as the Transactional Checklist, and taken with permission from *The Wellness Workbook,* by John Travis, Jr. and Regina Sara Ryan.

Mark each of the statements below as it applies to you, according to this code: 0=seldom or never; 1=sometimes or occasionally; and 2=frequently. (X=significant others in your life, such as spouse, boss, parents, friend, or colleague.)

___ 1. Is it hard for you to take time for yourself and have fun?

___ 2. Do you supply words for X when s/he hesitates?

___ 3. Do you set limits for yourself that you then exceed?

___ 4. Do you believe you are responsible for making (keeping) X happy?

___ 5. Do you enjoy lending a shoulder for X to "cry" on?

___ 6. Do you believe that X is not sufficiently grateful for your help?

___ 7. Do you take care of X more than you take care of yourself?

___ 8. Do you find yourself interrupting when X is talking?

___ 9. Do you watch for clues for ways to be helpful to X?

___ 10. Do you make excuses, openly or mentally, for X?

___ 11. Do you do more than your share, that is, work harder than X?

___ 12. When X is unsure or uncomfortable about doing something, do you do it for X?

___ 13. Do you give up doing things because X wouldn't like it?

___ 14. Do you find yourself thinking that you really know what is best for X?

___ 15. Do you think X would have grave difficulty getting along without you?

___ 16. Do you use the word "we" and then find you don't have X's consent?

___ 17. Do you stop yourself by thinking X will feel badly if you say or do something?

___ 18. Is it hard for you *not* to respond to anyone who seems hurting or needing help?

___ 19. Do you find yourself being resented when you were only trying to be helpful?

___ 20. Do you find yourself giving advice that is not welcome or accepted?

___ **Score.** More than 10 points, rescuing is possible; more than 20 points, rescuing is probable.

Bibliography

Melody Beattie. *Codependent No More: How to Stop Controlling Others and Start Caring for Yourself.* New York: Harper and Row, 1987. 230 pages. The author, a recovering alcoholic and former chemical dependency counselor, details the characteristics of codependency, where the behavior comes from, and how it affects us and those around us. She offers hope and guidance, discusses several options to control behavior, and helps you understand that *letting go* will set you free.

Melody Beattie. *Beyond Codependency and Getting Better All the Time.* San Francisco: Harper and Row, 1989. 252 pages. The author's second book moves beyond understanding codependency to explore the dynamics of recovery, the role "recycling" plays as a normal—even necessary—part of recovery, and how positive affirmations can counter negative messages. This book is for those who don't want just to survive but are ready to grow in the realization that recovery from codependency is a lifelong process.

Betty Berzon. *Permanent Partners: Building Gay and Lesbian Relationships That Last.* New York: E. P. Dutton, 1988. 354 pages. The author, a psychotherapist who specializes in working with same-sex couples, defines the issues and offers an array of options for dealing with them effectively. She has drawn on her fifteen years of professional experience to create a strategy for overcoming the obstacles faced by gay men and lesbians as they try to build healthy relationships. Some of the obstacles are the lack of visible long-term couples as role models; the absence of support from society—from employers, landlords, and insurers—and, too often, from a couple's families of origin; a "tradition of failure"; and the "guidance gap" with regard to how one builds a life with another man or another woman. The book offers new hope for the gay man or lesbian woman who thinks about being coupled.

Claudia Black. *Repeat After Me.* Denver: M.A.C. Printing and Publications, 1981. 154 pages. Troubled families produce troubled children. Troubled children grow into adults with living problems. This is a self-help book designed to provide the reader with a step-by-step program for overcoming those problems and beginning a healthier, happier lifestyle. The author walks the reader through the problems, explaining each aspect of the problem, then offers a series of exercises and suggestions to begin the wellness process.

Timmen L. Cermak. *Diagnosing and Treating Co-Dependence: A Guide for Professionals Who Work with Chemical Dependents, Their Spouses and Children.* Minneapolis: Johnson Institute Books, 1986. 111 pages. Dr. Cermak presents clear diagnostic criteria for co-dependency and illustrates them with examples. He describes new ways of treating co-dependence that go beyond the approaches currently in use.

John Friel and Linda Friel. *Adult Children: The Secrets of Dysfunctional Families.* Deerfield Beach, FL: Health Communications, Inc., 1988. 198 pages. The authors explore the experiences of children who grow up in dysfunctional families in which perfectionism, workaholism, compulsive overeating, intimacy problems, depression, or problems in expressing feelings produce a family system much like that of an alcoholic. The authors provide a readable explanation of what happened to you and how you can change.

Carol Gilligan. *In a Different Voice.* Cambridge: Harvard University Press, 1982. 184 pages. The author believes that the field of psychology has persistently and systematically misunderstood women—their motives, their moral commitments, the course of their psychological growth, and their special view of what is important in life. Developmental theories have traditionally been built on observations of men's lives. Gilligan attempts to correct psychology's misperceptions and refocus its view of female personality. The result reshapes our understanding of human experience. Her thesis is rooted in common sense. It is a persuasive account of female moral development and the female life cycle.

Herb Goldberg. *The Hazards of Being Male: Surviving the Myth of Masculine Privilege.* New York: Signet, 1977. 195 pages. Men have heard for as long as they can remember that it is a "man's world" and that they are the privileged sex. What they often discover too late is that their "privileges" include the right to live lives of mounting frustration, weariness, and loneliness, and to die earlier than their female counterparts. For American men are raised by parents, conditioned by society, and encouraged by women to play a role of lover-husband-parent-breadwinner-strong and silent man whose impossible demands psychically cripple and physically kill them early.

Louise L. Hay. *You Can Heal Your Life.* Santa Monica, CA: Hay House, 1984. 225 pages. The author, a metaphysical teacher and workshop leader who was once diagnosed with terminal cancer, says that "if you are willing to do the mental work, almost anything can be healed." She offers practical steps for dissolving both the fears and causations of diseases. She devotes her life to assisting others in discovering and using the full potential of their own creative powers.

Health Communications, Inc. *Co-dependency: An Emerging Issue.* Hollywood, FL, 1985. 91 pages. Several authors contributed articles for this book, which covers many issues related to alcoholism. There are chapters on sexuality, being addicted to the addict, personality disturbances, intimacy, and family warning signs of alcoholism.

Cheryl Hetherington. "Co-Dependency: An Issue for Female Therapists." *Journal of the National Association for Women Deans, Administrators, and Counselors* 51:1 (1987), pp. 17-21. The article presents a definition of co-dependency and discusses ways that female therapists may manifest co-dependent patterns in their work. The author provides suggestions for changing these behaviors so the therapist is healthier and her work with clients is more effective.

Elisabeth Kubler-Ross. *Death and Dying.* New York: Collier, 1969. 289 pages. The author, a medical doctor, psychiatrist, and internationally renowned thanatologist, brought death out of the darkness. She has helped thousands of people deal with personal losses by helping us see the grieving process as a healthy, natural one. She offers hope for the understanding of human strengths and weaknesses experienced during a difficult time.

Harriet Goldhor Lerner. *Dance of Anger: A Woman's Guide to Changing the Patterns of Intimate Relationships.* New York: Harper and Row, 1985. 239 pages. This book provides a helpful guide to understanding and reducing anger in close relationships by showing how anger works to maintain the status quo as well as to change it. Dr. Lerner, a psychotherapist at the Menninger Foundation, gives readers information they can use to manage anger wisely and well.

Harriet Goldhor Lerner. *Dance of Intimacy: A Woman's Guide to Courageous Acts of Change in Key Relationships.* New York: Harper and Row, 1989. 255 pages. Lerner takes a careful look at those relationships in which intimacy is most challenged by too much distance, too much intensity, or simply too much pain. She illustrates how you can move differently in these key relationships.

Ruth Maxwell. *The Booze Battle.* New York: Ballantine Books, 1980. 148 pages. This book is written for the spouse, partner, boss, or friend of the alcoholic. It is helpful to learn what to do to take better care of your own needs, to recover yourself from enabling or co-dependent patterns. You too can seek help, get more control of your life, be less blaming and angry, and become happier.

Stanton Peele. *Love and Addiction.* New York: Signet, 1975. 309 pages. This is one of the earliest books about the addictive nature of relationships. The author, a social psychologist, describes how people turn to one another or to alcohol and other drugs to meet needs. He talks of how addiction is really psychological, social and cultural; he presents clear guidelines for analyzing existing relationships in terms of their potential for mutual growth; and he provides insightful, step-by-step means of strengthening one's psychological center.

Lillian Rubin. *Intimate Strangers: Men and Women Together.* New York: Harper and Row, 1982. 222 pages. The book is for every woman and man who yearns for an intimate relationship with the other sex and wonders why it seems so elusive. She explains how gender differences affect such critical issues in adult relationships as intimacy, sexuality, dependency, work, and parenting. She writes of the "approach-avoidance dance" of intimacy, "redefining dependency," and "sexual dilemma."

Virginia Satir. *Peoplemaking.* Palo Alto, CA: Science and Behavior Books, Inc., 1972. 310 pages. An expert in family therapy, the author writes this engaging and interesting book about becoming a more nurturing parent. It is appropriate for the average family and provides a process for reviewing family patterns and guidelines for mapping a more nurturing family style. The book is a workbook with exercises families can use to learn new levels of family communication.

Anne Wilson Schaef. *Co-dependency: Misunderstood—Mistreated.* Minneapolis: Harper and Row, 1986. 105 pages. Co-dependency is defined as one form of what the author calls "the addictive process," an underlying, generic, primary disease whose assumptions, beliefs, and lack of spiritual awareness are openly supported by the society in which you live. She traces the history and development of the concept of co-dependence and discusses its often confusing, overlapping definitions.

Anne Wilson Schaef. *Escape from Intimacy.* San Francisco: Harper and Row, 1989. 165 pages. The author exposes and examines the problem of addictions to sex, romance, and relationships, clearly defining where healthy activities end and addictive behavior begins. This life-saving resource is for all those struggling to overcome "love" addictions—disorders that can destroy relationships and careers.

Barbara Sher. *Wishcraft: How to Get What You Really Want.* New York: Ballantine Books, 1979. 278 pages. The author offers effective strategies for making real change in your life. This human, practical program puts your vague yearnings and dreams to work for you—with concrete results. You will learn how to discover your strengths and skills, turn your fears and negative feelings into positive tools, diagram the path to your goal, and map out target dates for meeting it.

Bernie Siegel. *Peace, Love and Healing.* New York: Harper and Row, 1989. 290 pages. The emphasis of this book is on self-healing, the ability given to us by a creator and one ignored by medicine. Modern medicine and self-healing can be cooperative. The book challenges us, whether we are well or ill, to recognize how our mind influences our body and how to use this knowledge to our advantage.

John Travis and Regina Sara Ryan. *Wellness Workbook.* Berkeley, CA: Ten Speed Press, 1981, 1988. 236 pages. This book discusses new ways to think about personal responsibility and health. An invitation to take control of your health and life, the book provides tools to help you understand and to guide you to wellness— enduring good health. With hundreds of exercises and ideas plus a 300-item self-scoring questionnaire, "The Wellness Index," the goal is to put you in charge of ongoing and direct endeavor in which health is more than the absence of disease.

Sharon Wegscheider-Cruse. *Coupleship: How to Build a Relationship.* Deerfield Beach, FL: Health Communications, Inc., 1985. 151 pages. Forming a happy, joy-filled partnership is one of the greater challenges. Through this book you may find some ideas and tools to enhance a current marriage or partnership, make a decision about commitment, explore ways to find a partner, and learn about "romance responsibility," "romance invaders," sexuality, intimacy, and much more. Loving and being loved isn't a skill. It is a learned process sprinkled with a little magic. Explore, learn, and understand.

Sharon Wegscheider. *Another Chance: Hope and Health for the Alcoholic Family.* Palo Alto, CA: Science and Behavior Books, Inc., 1981. 256 pages. This is a helpful guide for physicians, counselors, lawyers, ministers, and other helping professionals who must deal with the difficult problems of alcoholics and their families. But its easy-to-read style and moving human stories invite the layperson, too, to share its message of hope. For the millions of Americans who suffer under the burden of their own or a loved one's alcoholism, it offers fresh insight on what is happening in their families and what they personally can do to change it.

Janet Geringer Woititz. *Adult Children of Alcoholics.* Pompano Beach, FL: Health Communications, Inc., 1983. 105 pages. Although originally written with children of alcoholics in mind, the material in this book applies to other types of dysfunctional families as well. If you did not grow up with alcoholism, but lived, for example, with other compulsive behaviors such as gambling, drug abuse, or overeating, or you experienced chronic illness, were adopted, lived in foster care, or in other potentially dysfunctional systems, you may find that you identify with the characteristics presented in the book.

Janet Geringer Woititz. *Struggle for Intimacy.* Pompano Beach, FL: Health Communications, Inc., 1985. 101 pages. A human relations counselor, the author writes about the struggles that adult children of alcoholics (ACOAs) have with intimate relationships. She defines a healthy relationship and discusses the difficulties—fear of abandonment and loss of self, bonding, anger, guilt, shame, depression, and control—that ACOAs have in finding and keeping healthy relationships.

About the Author

Cheryl Hetherington, Ph.D., is a licensed psychologist, training consultant and a university faculty member. She has published dozens of articles and presented nationwide on co-dependency, women's concerns, diversity, personality type, and grief. For over a decade she has practiced as a psychologist and educator. Dr. Hetherington is the founder of Hetherington and Associates, which provides therapy to individuals and couples. She presents training seminars thoughout the United States and teaches at the University of Iowa.

To order more books:

Write:
Hetherington & Associates
P.O. Box 367
Iowa City, Iowa 52244

Please send me _____copies of *Bring Your Self to Life at* $11.95 each. (Iowa residents add 4% sales tax.) Please add $2.00 to this order to cover postage and handling for one book and $.50 for each extra copy). Send check or money order—no cash or C.O.D.'s. I am enclosing $_____.

Please send to:
Name _____
Address _____
City _____State_____ Zip _____

Please send a copy to the following friends:

Name _____
Address _____
City _____State _____Zip _____

Name _____
Address_____
City_____ State _____ Zip_____

Name _____
Address_____
City _____ State _____ Zip_____

Allow 4-6 weeks for delivery.
This offer subject to withdrawal without notice.